In memory of Shelley Robin.

THE SENSITIVE VEIN

BY FRANCIS MARTINEAU

MOON DANCE
PUBLISHING

Book Design by Sutton Annas
Cover Design & Illustration by Sutton Annas

MOON DANCE Publishing, 2711 Orchard St., Soquel, Ca. 95073

Printed by McNaughton & Gunn, Saline, Mi. 48176
First Printing: September 1992

Library of Congress Cataloging-in-Publication Data

Martineau, Francis
The Sensitive Vein
1. Self-actualization (Psychology) 2. Self-actualization (Psychology)–Case studies. I. Title

BF637.S4M367 1991 158–dc20 92-81538
ISBN 0-9633082-0-3
PRINTED IN THE UNITED STATES OF AMERICA

Many remarkable people have been involved in the writing and publishing of this book. They know who they are and I am most indebted to them. As I look back on my life, they form an indissoluble chain of vital support and information: take one link away and the strength and continuity are broken. Whether they have been in the role of teacher to me or I have been in the role of teacher to them, I have come to recognize that there is finally little difference in the potency and necessity of the exchange. They have had faith in me at the right time and there is no greater blessing I could ask.

Thank you, one and all.

Part One. Learning

Part Two. Supporting

Part Three. Exploring

OPENING

The word 'sensitive' was applied to me many times as a child. At the time I would have liked to believe that it was a mark of distinction, a gesture of appreciation for those special qualities that distinguished me from other children. But the attitude was far from complimentary. On the contrary, its effect was to set me apart from all that was normal, to identify me, once and for all, as a stranger, and to usher in an overwhelming feeling of being alone. Besides, this 'sensitive' label was never applied directly. It was whispered mysteriously in corners, as if I were not supposed to find out the full extent of the damage it wrought, and it was accompanied by a hopeless, despairing tone, a heavy sense of doom. They had given up on me. I was different, and there was nothing anyone could do about it except endure my peculiar behavior and keep it under some kind of reasonable control. Clearly I did not know how to go by the rules of life they had laid down, and I was never going to learn. What disturbed them most were my extreme reactions to situations and people around me. This unpredictable behavior became increasingly a source of embarrassment to others, while to myself it was a continuous reminder of the unacceptable nature of my disease.

Somehow I managed. I became invisible as much as possible. I tried to hide the more obvious symptoms of my strangeness. But my biggest discovery was adaptation. I adapted and I adapted again. I became good at it, so good that, in certain circumstances, I could put on an act of belonging that was convincing to everyone. Like a chameleon, I learned to move from one situation to another and always give the impression that each one was my true home. There came a time, still later, when I began to believe in my own act, believe in the fact that I had finally left this stigma of sensitivity behind me. I even convinced myself that I had found an easy way of dealing with the world that had seemed for so long to be an alien place; and as I reached the threshold of adulthood, I discovered, to my relief, that the 'sensitive' label was no longer being applied. Another word had taken its place: 'adaptable'. A very different tone accompanied this word, an encouraging tone, as if being adaptable were something I ought to be proud of, something that would be of great advantage to me as I made my way out into the world.

It took me a long time to find out what I lost on the road between 'sensitive' and 'adaptable' and how much my display of sensitivity was maligned during those early parts of my life. During those lonely years it never once occurred to me that it might be my most valued possession, the strongest part of my identity as an individual human being. But I had learned my skills of adaptation well, and I saw no advantages to opening myself all over again. So I remained closed, denying that there was anything I had missed out on.

It was fortunate, for all the denial, that I left a path open by which I could return. It was a circuitous route, but it served its purpose nonetheless. At the age of eighteen I took on my first job as teacher and found out that, even at so young an age, it came quite naturally to me. This meant that, from then on, I never had to look further for a career. It also meant that I was compelled, as all natural teachers are, to spend a lifetime finding out about myself through others. For years I taught what I myself had to learn, drawing out a hidden sensitivity from others well before I was able to recover and recognize the full wealth of it in myself. It was all, at first, a very slow process monitored by the fact that the subjects I taught kept changing. It was my way of being drawn back to the innermost core that I had abandoned as a child. I began with Greek and Latin, went on to English and European literature, specialized in American novels for a while, changed again to drama and practical theater, then finally found the ideal resolution: a way of teaching that had no labels attached to it at all. Each phase brought me closer to the naked human being, both in myself and in others, to the power that lay behind the masks and the posturing, to the center where the shattered sensitivity gave clear, if muffled, signals that it was still alive. My teaching and my discoveries about myself traveled hand in hand, the one informing the other along the way and both leading back to those voices that had whispered in corners about the strange doings of that sensitive child.

First of all, I found out that I was not the only one. In fact there were many of us, all lying low because of the same ignorant, suspicious voices, and all keeping hidden inside the remarkable perceptive and creative powers with which we were born. Whether we knew it or not, we had formed a conspiracy of secrecy and, for some reason, were reluctant to share what we knew. As teacher I moved in little by little, wanting access to those hidden parts of my students and finding encouragement in surprising flashes of inspiration. I was able to identify a new quality of life in those flashes, but they were gone before I could take in what it was they really wanted to say. I did not understand immediately, but this was my first experience of the sensitive nature's true expression. Quivering and afraid, it was waiting for enough safety to be released from its long-term confinement. I felt the purity of its energy and knew that, without its release, all my teaching efforts would be wasted. I could continue to offer knowledge on any number of subjects, but there would be no deep impact until the sensitivity in its fearful state was first given some attention. In the process of this discovery, it became increasingly obvious that I needed to take more risks, to be a catalyst, rather than just an expert in my field. But I could only do that if I were prepared to come to terms with my own fearful sensitivity and all that I had kept hidden from myself and others for so long. So a catalyst I became, but not without a great deal of floundering around. It was a messy business. I opened and my students opened in response. The flashes of inspiration became more sustained, and a new kind of liveliness began bouncing around.

This book begins, then, with the history of a joint movement into the unknown. I kept insisting on the unknown because I knew that what was already familiar would only get in the way, knew that what we were searching for bore little resemblance to anything that had already been found. Old forms had already been imposed, adaptations made long ago, and they had to be removed before anything new could begin. In fact, I found that the process of adaptation I had experienced as a child was rife in us all, and what had been sacrificed was an originality that lay deep at the core of each and every one of us. I became more fully aware of the extent of this sacrifice when practical theater became the subject of my teaching, but even before that, from school to different school, from courses in Greek to seminars in American literature, I was constantly nagged by this sense of straight-jacketed potential. And when the gold mine of theater became my ally, it finally dawned on me that the institutions I had been a part of for so long could not take me where I wanted to go. They were concerned with abstract knowledge, while I was concerned with human experience, and the gap between the two was growing wider all the time. Meanwhile, as I muddled along, I learned that a very specialized environment was going to have to be created if the deepest parts of this hidden nature were going to find their way to the surface again. For one thing the fear level was intense, and I knew I was not going to be able to address this emotional aspect, or any other, until I discovered a completely new teaching frame.

So I left the limits of institutions behind me in order to find out what this new frame was to be. I set myself up without subject-matter, without labels, and without any kind of advance expectations to confine me. I found a way to be with people, uncluttered by my previous academic background. What this entailed was the creation of an environment within which any kind of emotional improvisation could be encouraged, freedom of expression for all those who had been forced to close down as children when their sensitivity had come under attack. By developing a thorough system of support, which is described in the book's second section, I was able to confirm what I had suspected for some time: a unique, complex nature lies hidden in all of us with the desire to find its true range of expression again. However, this desire could only be activated by providing deep levels of safety and making no attempt to define or control the re-emerging process. The basic requirement was a trust in the individual nature which, through the very exercise of its freedom, would find the shape of its own identity again.

Recovering our sensitivity means opening for the first time to the mystery and strength of our natures as separate human beings. This is a process that for much of life has been associated with constant crisis, with a series of fearful and overwhelming events outside our control. More often than not, it involves opening to parts of ourselves that closed down before we were even aware of their existence. We were prevented from claiming them because of the accompanying cruelty and pain. So it takes a large shift, indeed a leap of faith, to believe that this process of opening can act to our advantage, that it is a natural, ongoing process of taking in more and more of ourselves through the daily experience of life. The act of closing down originally took over as an instinctive habit of protection, a necessary one for the child's survival. The child in us is still terrified at the idea of change, even though the adult may now be prepared to accept the consequences; but it is the child's terror that must be acknowledged first of all, and accepted without reservation. The disorientation of all this can be extreme indeed, given the amount of openness that is possible when permission is given to go all the way. We need foolproof support to ride the waves of this disorientation because we have been warned from an early age to go for the known rather than the unknown, to latch onto security whenever we get the chance. In a sense we have to begin again, to wheel around and set off in the opposite direction from the one to which we have been guided, or rather misguided, in the past. Only then can we grasp how many alternatives exist that before were not available to us. What the support offers is a new energy field to welcome these fresh alternatives and counteract the powerlessness of past experiences when all unusual exploration was cut short. The support synchronizes with a natural, birth-given need for expansion, assuring us that all directions are now open and this time we will not be restrained.

In this new territory there are no models to guide us, nothing that binds us comfortingly to a right or appropriate way of dealing with this turbulence, particularly if it takes us by surprise. At this stage there is little we can take from the outside and apply to the inside in a way that will offer any satisfying solution. Details may fit, but nothing provides a complete answer or can match the growing complexity of who we are becoming on the inside. Besides, there is the confusion of never quite knowing, from moment to moment, who we are. Identity keeps shifting as new discoveries are made and new elements enter in. The more we move into the unfamiliar, the more we have to do away with what others have offered us as appropriate models of behavior. For each being has its own rhythms and its own order and that individual order is only discoverable when all imposed rhythms are laid aside. It is a matter of risking what happens when they are laid aside, when the sensitive core is touched again, touched in a way that gives it courage to re-emerge rather than shrink away as it has been long accustomed to doing. Once the original confidence returns, then the inner journey can take up its direction again. The unfathomable in life becomes accessible without the anxiety of right and wrong and without the impotence of unending fear. It is a matter of understanding that the only certainty is the certainty of change and to resist it is to die a little all the time. Blockages build up in the system that prevent the life force from making its creative urges known. And the forms that have been imposed on us, whatever their origin, represent a subtle conspiracy against change, impressing on us the need for stability and uniformity in an unnatural attempt to stem the in-coming tide. All these forms have to be taken apart, and this can only be done in an atmosphere that encourages the natural flow of things and restores the belief that we have ample resources inside of us to deal with whatever comes our way.

The final section of the book explores aspects of the journey itself: its hazards, it extremes, and its rewards. It shows, once trust is established and the depths stirred, how much new ground there is to be covered, how little we have been prepared for life as children compared to the inner resources that could from the beginning have been at our beck and call. Life is not simple or easy at the best of times, yet most of us have not been allowed to develop even the most basic equipment with which to handle it all: essential foundations like an awareness of our own beauty, the freedom to express openly how we feel, or confirmation that the way people see us is not as important as who we really are. It is not surprising, given this dearth of equipment, that the need for security is so urgent and the more risky ventures so rare. To be alive is to have the freedom to experiment with all the qualities that make us who we are. And it is impossible to do that when we have no contact with those qualities and are prevented from getting in touch with them by the paralyzing fears of the past. From the physical sensation of aliveness comes the strength to go against the pattern of what is around us, the courage to set out and find the configuration that really belongs. We have to recover the energy required to follow our individual design as it keeps changing and leading us into the next unknown.

Year after year this journey can be delayed. Often it feels too deep, too disturbing to the familiar patterns already established. To be different as a child in the face of family and society has already caused trouble that was too much to bear. Why should the adult fare any better? The differences have been buried for years now, the extremes of nature forced underground and the range of expression increasingly narrowed down. Better that it should all stay that way. After all, being adaptable has its advantages. Yet the creative spirit is all the time fading inside, sacrificing itself to the adaptable mode. At some point a choice has to be made between allowing the sacrifice and making a bid to be free; between accepting the safety of the familiar and allowing the challenge of the unpredictable to stir us again; between holding on to the fear of the child and risking those extreme elements that may lead to a less acceptable mode of being in the world. Underneath it all, we have to discover that those differences are there to support us, not bring us down. And even if they will never offer a great deal of outer security, they will certainly make out of life the adventure it was always meant to be. What this book presents, in all its parts, is a frame for this adventure to become possible again, a way of reminding us how much we have been missing all these years and what it is like to assume the fullness of our lives once more. •

Part One. Learning

I. THE FULL RANGE

Like many of my generation, I was landed with a fixed moral code before I could even crawl. There was no waiting to find out what kind of child I was or consideration for what I might want to choose for myself as the experience of life entered in. The rules were already established and there was nothing I could do to change them. Yet if I were to attempt to describe my sensitive nature in its original state, I would portray it as more or less opposite in character to that fixed moral frame. I would see it as something subtle and fluid, a delicate instrument that, from the moment of its birth, requires delicate tuning as a form of homage to its unique character and tone. I would also assume that it needs time to grow and develop, time to discover its own identity as it responds freely to different people and different situations in life.

So the meeting between the new-born sensitivity and the already established moral code is bound to cause immediate problems. What is distinctly open and individual by nature is confronted by an attitude that is authoritarian and closed. Unfortunately the impact of the one on the other goes very deep. The sensitivity, much as it would like to resist such alien information, is infinitely impressionable and knows neither how to fend off the beliefs of others nor how to communicate the specialness of its own vision. There is a large difference between belief and vision. The one limits the imagination, while the other creates the desire to find out new things. If belief gets in before vision, the natural powers of perception and inspiration become confused, losing confidence in their capacity to integrate experience and make of it something significant and whole. The vision of a child is a very fragile thing, and it does not take very much external pressure to disturb its subtle manner of perceiving or force it to retreat from its vivid, fertile imaginings. The pressure is strong and once that moral code has entered in, it is hard to get free, hard to bring back the full range of life so that it becomes accessible again. The sensitivity becomes stifled and will not breathe easily again until the fixity of that single imposed belief lets go of its hold. The being can only come alive in proportion to the loosening of this hold, in proportion to the release into what we were told were unspeakable blasphemies and taboos. The sensitive nature needs all the raw material of life at its fingertips so that it can finally make up its own mind about the workings of the world, discover for itself the pattern of the universal design.

Perhaps the most discouraging aspect of any moral code is the impression given that there is a limit to what we can find out. Its very purpose is to create limitations, to wrap the truth up in a neat package, to provide answers and leave them be, to thwart the curious and imaginative impulse that would like to enquire further. To the sensitive child this is like a death knell because the natural instinct towards movement and change is curtailed almost before it has begun. The infinite has already become finite, the wide range of alternatives drastically whittled down.

Only in retrospect can I gather the full effect these restrictions had on me as a child. For example, time went unbearably slowly, which is not surprising when one considers that the time frame I was given had nothing to do with my own desires. Compared to now, it was an endless continuum, impossibly aimless and dull. Even if things changed on the outside, no significant movement happened on the inside, so I gradually became resigned to the fact that inner motion was not a part of life. Certain fixed values were set up and the being had to go along with them, regardless of what its own particular rhythms might be. I gave up believing that I could influence change in any way with the result that what was geared towards expansion and exploration in me closed down. It was horrifyingly simple. There were no alternatives. Things just stayed the same. Worst of all, I began to believe in this state of affairs, this one-dimensional view of the world, as if it were the only possible view anyone could hold.

To unfix myself, to break the stasis, to reclaim my vision out of this tangle of imposed beliefs, was a major operation that took many years. However, I can clearly remember the unassuming moment when it really began, when my mind was sufficiently jolted into beginning the search for those alternatives I had left behind so many years ago. It happened, strangely enough, with the reading of my first American novel, Hawthorne's *The Scarlet Letter*. It was an interesting experience because, unlike other novels I had read, I could not, for the longest time, get beyond the first chapter. I read it over and over, mystified and fascinated at the same time, not understanding what it was that had caught me. It was as if there were some hidden code inscribed within it that lurked just beyond the reaches of my mind. This chapter did not deal with the beginnings of narrative action or the introduction of characters; it simply focused on a description of two components of the setting, a wild rose and a prison. It described them in some detail, then left them there, two images hanging in space, seduced by a surprisingly sensual language into some kind of mysterious relationship with each other. I was given no connection to anything else. Even when I eventually continued with the rest of the novel and became caught up in the story that was told, the sense of mystery prevailed. There was a sense that however much was being defined or revealed, equally as much was being kept from me, was being elusively veiled. Yet I did not feel that this ambivalence was a deliberate tease. Hawthorne seemed to be using it as an instrument of investigation, a way of probing into the unfathomable nature of life without resolving it. Nothing, he appeared to be saying, is separate from anything else. Even if, for the sake of momentary clarity, two elements are set up as opposite in nature from each other, some kind of kinship is bound eventually to emerge between them. All this was conveyed more as a sensory impression than a philosophical idea and what came from it was an inner, poetic version of reality that took on much greater power than any moral code, even the harsh Puritan version that Hawthorne was using as the foundation of his tale. Poetic vision came face to face with moral judgment and was determined not to be put down. This was a very new idea for me at the time, accustomed as I had been to reading English or European novels that announced very clearly the moral premises with which they were dealing. If they set up situations of conflict in the opening pages, they were sure to resolve them in one way or another by the end. But there was no more a resolution at the end of *The Scarlet Letter* than there had been in the opening chapter; so I could only conclude that, according to Hawthorne, nothing in life was resolvable, no moral premises reliable or firm. From there I went on to immerse myself in other American novelists and found much the same story. My limited territory had been taken by storm and there was no turning back.

This was all very much a mental process and a long time elapsed before this influence made its impact in a more personal way. Indeed it is fascinating how much the mind can take in before it decides to filter it through to the inner emotional layers. As an academic these ideas fascinated me and I incorporated them into my teaching with gusto, giving lively voice to this love affair with American literature for a considerable number of years. But it was all theory, disembodied and unconnected to any other dimension in my life. It was only when I changed my focus to theater that I discovered how to apply these discoveries to my teaching in a constructive way. I designed an introductory theater course that posed the basic question, 'what is theater?'. I formed it around six major practitioners in the field, chosen for their extreme views and for their completely different ideas on what gave theater its power. I immersed my students in each of them, one by one. We spent enough time with each figure for them to thoroughly identify with his particular style; then as soon as they were hooked and convinced that this one approach was the only way, we would move on to the next, who proceeded to contradict everything that had already been established. I usually encountered some resistance during the transition period, but a new quality of energy gradually took hold as this next approach found its own ground. When immersion was complete in this area, we shifted again. At each shift there was resistance until, eventually, a deeper form of confusion set in. It was at this point that the course really got underway. Each opposing view made the initial question about the nature of theater more impossible to answer, with the result that the students were increasingly thrown back on their own resources. The theories that I had initially imposed from the outside gradually lost any authority they might once have had and gave way to an internal place of deep questioning. It was a fascinating process to be a part of because untapped resources had to be tapped for the first time and the students were compelled to take on their own visions of what the theater could do. The outside was taken over by the inside as they accepted the challenge of contradictions and allowed their original decisions about the nature of theater to be overthrown.

Year after year this course was a catalyst for deep change, and eventually I was ready to analyse the reasons for this change more closely. The design of the course certainly made a strong contribution, but there was no question that my interaction with the students played an equally important role. Looking at this in more detail, I saw that what Hawthorne had originally done for me as a writer I was now doing for my students as teacher. I was setting up some clarity of design as a means of entry, then shifting and expanding the boundaries as soon as entry was made. Clear polarities were set up at the outset, but in a way that allowed for movement, that made room for new relationships and combinations to form and constantly reform. There also had to be room for the outer form to move towards its inward reflection. Generally students came into the course with some fixed idea on what theater was for them, but they were not aware that their conclusions had engaged only a fraction of their total being. Ideas from experts in the field gave them the means whereby they could reach beyond their own limitations, but the more important function of this design was to give them something to hold onto while they launched into space, launched into the unexplored areas of themselves. By engaging in these extreme views they were already, without their knowledge, being projected into a more volatile, fluid, personal motion. Old patterns of belief broke down, preparing the way for a more inward journey. Sometimes I could feel this movement as something palpable, like a sudden circulation of fresh air. At other times I could feel waves of fear as some kind of resistance took over, informing me that an objective grappling with ideas was developing into more personal concerns. Then there were also moments when the movement and the fear seemed to hang there together, suspended, uncertain as to which would hold sway. Whatever the dynamic, I knew that I was touching on something that went beyond their commitment to theater, something that was closer to a commitment to themselves and all the doubts and uncertainties that inevitably followed along.

For example, when fear entered, the range of exploration was immediately curtailed. If we were searching on uncertain ground, an instant need arose to return to what was familiar. All at once old definitions were called in as emergency replacement, a language that was usually full of automatic words and phrases which, through constant repetition, had had all the meaning squeezed out of them. They would come rushing in along with the fear and clamp down on what it was we were really searching for, taking all energy away from the discussion and leaving us empty and cold. This was necessary, I realized, to avoid the insecurity of not knowing. It was too exposing to be inarticulate and stumble around. So one important role I played was to identify this invasion of lifelessness and insist that we let ourselves stumble around. It was in this way that I first found the extraordinary power of silence, because silence was what often came over us as soon as we let the inarticulateness hold. I got used to prolonging these quiet periods for as long as it took the open space of exploration to return, feeling at the same time how fragile it was for a group of people to admit to their ignorance, to not be able to sink back on the safety of familiar ideas. In those lone moments, I made palpable contact with that uncomfortable passage from the outside to the inside. I was equally aware of how the fear remained as a glaring, unwelcome part of it all.

There was another role I played, however, that was more difficult to define because it touched so directly on my own limitations. If I were asking for open space, then it obviously began with me, with my flexibility and my willingness to move in any direction so as not to block the new combinations of thought emerging. Open space meant that I got myself out of the way, and getting myself out of the way meant being able to welcome all varieties of response to the subject at hand, however outlandish they might initially appear. Above all, it meant acknowledging my own state of unknowing, especially when new territory was being explored. I had to waive any sense of right and wrong; for as soon as I became an authority of that kind, I was simply replacing one limited framework with another and not allowing the new discoveries to be given the freedom they deserved. It was all a matter of doing away with preconceptions, avoiding any premature conclusions about the capabilities of the students. The more I was able to do this, the more I was taken by surprise. Time and again I was shown that to be with people in the process of change was to be completely ignorant of who they could become when one or another of their limitations fell away. Like Hawthorne, I was only there to keep the richness of the given elements moving, to keep suggesting relationships between things that had not already been noted so that the full scope of the material could be explored. And, more often than not, I found myself in the way. I could not get used to the range of different individual's responses to the same thing. I could not adapt myself fast enough to the extremes of opinion that clamored around me. I would go to meet one person in a way that I felt matched the energy coming towards me and the necessary information would circle without obstruction; then I would meet another in the same way and find myself utterly at a loss, unable to find any freedom of exchange.

The whole process, the hit and miss aspect of it, mystified me and forced me to come to terms with how distinctly individual each person was and what a range I had to call on in my own being to find each appropriate form of meeting. I was out of my depth most of the time, and all I could do was keep track of the increasing complexity and note the acute discomfort of certain people with whom I established only the most tenuous lines of communication.

Yet over the years enough students came my way to show me the potential for a very intimate form of meeting. Where there was a willingness on both our sides to really open, the results were undeniable, giving me my first glimpse of the contrast between the surface of a human being and what was possible once the hidden depths were stirred. Through their examples I was challenged to discover more, to imagine what would happen if I had a chance to investigate human nature on its own footing without having to use theater, or any other external reference point, as an intermediary. What I saw when the deepest changes occurred and the inner nature began to take on its power was something that reminded me of that first reading of *The Scarlet Letter.* I saw the possibility of life without categories or compartments or judgments. I saw it become more and more like a musical flow, mysterious, untranslatable, yet with all the mixing of moods that music can offer, dark and light flashing in and out of one another, joy and pain finding their roots together.

But first I needed a more physical manifestation of all this, and it was convenient that I was able to turn to the practical side of theater for the next stage of my teaching career. In this way I was able to set myself and my students in motion and peel off the next layer.

•

II. THE CREATIVE IMPULSE

The advantage of theater—and one of the reasons why I moved under its influence after studying and teaching literature for so long—is that there must always be a physical side. And once the physical becomes fully engaged, a whole different quality of change becomes possible. When I began to teach practical theater, I leapt in one single bound from my head into my body, from passive into active, and from the limits of words into the open field of improvisation. In that one large shift I was brought closer to the inner workings of human nature and, above all, closer to the emotional response that is inevitable when there is a strong urge for creative expression. There was also a more concrete challenge, for this was not a subject that lent itself easily to organized structure. I could not plan the courses in advance, although at first I attempted to do so by giving the students set scripts and asking them to play out a succession of roles from different historical periods. The results were unsatisfying, to say the least. Forced into unnatural poses and defeated by their own expectations of what performance ought to be, they found little dramatic life in the roles or themselves. They showed a confusing mixture of being in touch with something really alive and being caught in an extended artifice from which there seemed no release.

Given all this, I realized I had to go back to the very beginning, back to the place where nothing was taken for granted and nothing imposed by the opinions of so-called experts in the field. I threw out all texts, all words, all set speeches, and began to work entirely with the raw potential of the human body and voice. I had a hunch that all movement came from a spontaneous impulse if I could only track it back that far, if I could only take away all preconceptions of what 'acting' was supposed to be. This meant that, whenever anyone began to move or make a sound, there had to be a direct connection to the individual's own creative source. Yet there were so many other influences that had been superimposed and so much that had to be cut away before this kind of spontaneous energy could emerge. I did not, at the time, understand the origin of this interference, but I certainly knew it was a severe hindrance in what we had to do. So I kept going back to the beginning and checking those initial impulses again and again, evolving over the years a unique improvisatory style. This was not the kind of improvisation that made use of set situations or pre-suggested ideas. It simply began with an initial physical impulse and went from there, each moment finding its inspiration from the one before and so developing organically its own natural design. I wooed this spontaneous impulse out of hiding and insisted that it take the lead in everything, create its own flow of images outside the realm of conscious understanding.

But there always came a time, as the course neared its end, when some kind of performance was required. I grew to dread that moment more and more because, in order for the show to be given adequate preparation, a break had to be made from the improvisatory process. And as the imposed form closed in, I could see the life we had created in the previous months, slowly ebbing away. However much I tried to bridge the gap, this precious life kept slipping away, leaving behind only a fraction of the spontaneity that I had nurtured so carefully. Then one year a group of students made a momentous decision. They decided collectively that they would not let the need of a performance interfere with their discoveries in improvisation but would rather take the risk of performing that way. They would continue to improvise in front of an audience and find out if the spontaneity of its energy could be sustained under such intense exposure. In this way I was able to move on to the next stage of experimentation and find out what a direct, visceral form of communication was contained within this spontaneous performing style, how the presence of an audience added extra impetus for the creative energy to become fuller still.

The details of this development over the years are not important here, but the core discoveries are. At the center of the work was a ruthless cutting away of habit, a stripping away of all gestures and sounds which had become engrained in the system and prevented the true nature from being exposed. It was fascinating to observe what happened when all familiar associations were taken away, when the students ventured into an open space with no preconception of what they were going to do or where they were going to begin. At certain moments they would be seized by a total paralysis, and from that paralyzed state repeat automatic gestures compulsively over and over again; while at other moments they would be taken over by a rush of invention that took us all completely by surprise. The inspiration might last a few seconds only, yet those few seconds were enough for some new energy to enter in; because a few months later, those same students might be sustaining that spontaneity for half an hour or more, keeping unbroken contact with an urge that created extended scenarios out of nothing but their own moment-to-moment discoveries.

To help break through those states of paralysis and the habits they had already formed, I developed a series of exercises for the voice and body. All of them were an attempt to extend the range of expression available, to encourage the physical being into unfamiliar extensions. Through these extremes of pose and gesture I wanted the students, as much as possible, to become unrecognizable to themselves. I insisted on extremes so that they would feel the range of possibility within them, and during the process of improvisation, each impulse was exhorted to its furthest limits. I soon discovered that indecisive impulses never had any power behind them, and I spent a great deal of time identifying the difference between those impulses that lost confidence mid-projection and those that went all the way. I also had to expose all forms of imitation, half-hearted copies of models that they had picked up along the way, or even, perhaps, of certain people who had acted as major influences in their lives. It was hard to tell exactly from where these images came, but it was not hard to distinguish between the imitation and the real thing. The one projected no energy at all, while the other was alive from the moment the impulse gave it life. There were layers within layers of defense and automation before the intention and force of the impulse became clear. Some were able to go deep very fast, while there were others whose fear of exposure was so great that they could hardly make any headway at all. They hung onto their automated routines with such fervor that I wondered if they would not prefer to die rather than let them be taken over by a more original force. In these extreme situations, my only recourse was to keep working with them physically in an exhaustive way, knowing that much of the mental hysteria was broken down in the process. With a range of physical exercises I stretched their bodily and vocal potential to the limit, then moved directly into improvised action before they could forget the new surge of information. During the early stages of the work some sessions were continuous stop and go, no more than a few seconds of sustained action at one time, so determined was I to let nothing foreign interfere with the genuine life I could feel waiting to come through.

This work developed in me an intensity of concentration I had never experienced before. It was this singleness of purpose that must have generated between the students and I such a generous portion of trust. I have no other way to explain the amount that we risked over the years, how tenaciously we held onto our belief in the renewal of certain resources once the old were emptied away. It was true that the physical being was initially very reluctant to come forward with all it had to offer, expressing a kind of despair of emptiness before it could make the leap into the new. But when it appeared most empty was the time when it showed itself most full, and it was in those moments of despair that the deepest discoveries were often made. It was the presence of an audience that gave us the necessary evidence here because the challenge and the fear grew to such an extreme pitch together. The results of this experiment were not consistent by any means. In fact, there were times when a collective fear completely paralyzed the proceedings, cutting off all spontaneous energy from the performance. Then out of the void, out of the emergency of the situation, there suddenly sprang extraordinary moments of invention that had no logical explanation to them at all. It was as if fear had to freeze the mind before the pure impulse could come through. As an observer I loved it because, despite the possibility of a total energy failure, I had no idea what was going to happen next, no idea who was going to reveal something of themselves in a completely new way. For the students the experience of an audience was the ultimate risk, and most admitted that after putting themselves night after night on the line in this way, they were never the same again. The truth was they knew they were capable of anything once they had put their resources to the test with such complete abandon. They experienced both the extremity of the risk and the thrill of spontaneous moments that carried them away into quite unpredictable flights of improvisation; for there were almost always moments of intense audience contact that gave them a taste of their new-found powers. Such immediate contact with an audience seemed to reach into hidden recesses and impel them into action before any kind of defense could close them in. I knew then that something large was happening, knew that we were touching on some vital creative center that I had never seen touched before. And those moments only happened when the creative channels were completely cleared and given access to an inexhaustible well.

What was equally striking was how, within the intensity of the performing atmosphere, the identity of each actor found a sudden clarity and definition. It was like a colorful range of acting styles developing before my eyes, the form finally able to contain the spontaneity without cutting off its natural life. It was justification of the many approaches I used in the preparation work as a means of counteracting the students' resistance and fear. For in my move from the mental to the physical realm, I had greatly extended my ability to identify and deal with the more volatile aspects of the work. A new sensory language made itself known to me, and I found it a much more effective means of contact where any kind of resistance was concerned. The subtleties of this language I learned as the years went on, and they were refined through closer and closer powers of observation. Observation is perhaps not quite the right word; it was more like a feeling sense of what was different in people and what would help those distinctive qualities to feed the creative in them. In this context words were surprisingly limited. I found myself speaking very little, making contact instead through touch or through the eyes or by blending in physically with what they were doing. All this involved tuning in sensorily to how each individual moved, using my physical presence as a way of grounding and detailing what was going on. Words were not encouraged as an ingredient of improvisation either. If they entered in at all, it was only to do with a later stage of development, once the body had found its full physical projection. Words only seemed to work if they found a deep sensory source of their own; otherwise they took away life and carrying power from the physical action. I also observed how the strength of group improvisation depended on a very precise form of physical listening, how the simple presence of one performer next to another could act as an energetic linkage for the collective imagination to keep moving, a passing on of information that was quite invisible to the naked eye.

I finally had to acknowledge that the creative impulse could, in the spur of the moment, come up with anything; that there was an infinite store of invention lying dormant in the unconscious which only had to be given a decisive signal of encouragement to find its way into conscious expression. The form did not need an elaborate artifice in advance, but could act with lightening speed in giving shape to the expression as it emerged. If the impulse was clear and the focus strong, an appropriate form embraced it effortlessly. Then, with the introduction of a fresh impulse, the rhythms changed and with them the form also. The more the source was tapped, the more it had to offer. But if the source were cut off, if the fears took over, paralysis could set in at a moment's notice, and it was the contrast between the paralysis and the flow that showed me how severe was the curb on the creative urges within us. The physical being so wanted to fly, was so eager to demonstrate its expressive powers; yet the system had also been given information from somewhere that it was very dangerous to take the attempt too far.

So the limitlessness that I had already experienced in the realm of the mind obviously belonged to the physical imagination also, as long as the fears did not take hold. But the fears **did** take hold, and the unpredictable nature of the whole process continued to mystify me. Everything seemed to be poised on such a delicate edge, and I finally had no control over whether the balance could be sustained by the required consistency of creative flow. One night of performance could produce an uninterrupted hour of glorious invention, leaving the audience gasping and longing for more; then the following night everything could freeze within five minutes, leaving the actors and the audience embarrassed, both utterly at a loss and barely able to go on stumbling through. How could such confidence be there one moment and so completely gone the next? To answer this question was clearly my next challenge, and I knew it involved coming to terms with a whole new level of human nature, a level that, perhaps, was not accessible through the medium of the theater. I began to recognize that, even if I went on doing improvised shows for years to come, this particular problem would not be solved. Besides, by this time, theater had become too separated from life, and within my present teaching environment I could not see a way to bridge the two. The subject-matter of theater had locked me in. All the changes in people I had been witness to, even though they had a deeply personal resonance, were still dependent on its seductive draw. I saw how theater released the hidden impulses and was a vehicle through which a new kind of energy could be born, but I could not find where that energy touched upon the more natural process of living, upon situations that had no bearing on performance at all. I wanted to close the gap and knew that I would have to leave theater for a while in order to do so. Besides, for some time I had felt a new form of perception emerging from this work. It did not seem to be a part of the mind or the body and, perhaps for that reason, I had been reluctant to give it full play. I also knew instinctively that this hold-back was a large part of the impasse in my theater work, and if I was going to find out more about it, my field of operations would have to radically change.

III. THE INTUITIVE SENSE

I did not have to wait long for this change to happen. I resigned from the University where I had been teaching for sixteen years and went to a retreat center for an open-ended stay. There I met a woman who helped me identify and develop this quality of perception that, during the last period of my theater teaching, had begun to make itself known. She was the resident 'psychic' and had a reputation that inspired a potent mixture of fear and respect within the community. Rumors flew thick and fast around her and my initial reaction was to steer clear of her sphere of influence. The so-called psychic realm had never held much attraction for me anyway, associating it as I did with the shady dealings of eccentric people and unreliable predictions about the future. However, through an unusual sequence of events, I found myself in a group she was teaching and right away had to own up to the narrowness of my views. Within minutes I was admitting to myself that my suspicions had been unfounded and was opening without resistance to the extraordinary nature of what she had to say.

It was unlike anything I had experienced before. She had a method of working that involved a form of automatic writing in response to questions. She asked everyone in turn to address questions to her about their concerns; then before they had even finished speaking, wrote with great speed on a notepad in front of her, keeping the pen in continuous contact with the paper until she was done. But it was her voice, when she read aloud what she had written, that carried the most power. It had a strong oratorical resonance and an acute awareness of the appropriate intonation of each individual word. There was nothing flashy or showmanlike about the process at all; in fact, what came through was a depth of insight that moved me like a fine poem. I had not expected poetry, and to hear it in a form that connected to the inner layers of people's psyches was an altogether new combination. The answers to each question were not only imaginative and perceptive, but made use of the power of her tone to penetrate through to what had been buried in people for a long time. She moved directly to the most tender places, stripping people down to their core before they were even aware of what was going on. As she continued on her round, answering one question after another in this probing poetic style, a kind of emotional pandemonium began to fill the room. It was an inner, almost silent panic as everyone flailed around, taken off guard by such a sudden assault on their souls. The poetic style had a way of bypassing the workings of the mind which did not stand a chance, however fast they operated in protest against what she was saying. All in all, she stirred things up royally and, after three hours, there was nobody in the room who was not touched by the changes that had transpired.

I had been admitted to the group as an observer only, so I asked no questions of my own and was able to stay well outside of the emotional vortex. As far as I was concerned, everything she had spoken was brilliantly clear; my response was sheer excitement, not fear, tuned in as I was to a new, but strangely familiar communication wave. Indeed there were times when I found myself almost anticipating what she was going to say in answer to each question, as if a part of me knew in advance the kind of contact she was trying to find. I was able to see each individual through her perceptions and recognize both the truth of who they were and the channel she was searching for through which to reach them. The excitement of this discovery was further accentuated by streaming sensations in my body that I had never felt before. Clearly my understanding was coming from a physical rather than an intellectual source. The words seemed to connect to a feeling space in each person, and the effect was like a deep shaking of the system, different for each individual concerned. By aligning with her so closely I was able to feel that difference and know how essential it was to be able to make contact at such a core level. Most important of all was the discovery that such contact was possible within myself. I became aware that this way of seeing and feeling was communicable and had the power to reach the foundations of people's lives. Her pad of paper and her looped writing style I knew did not belong to me; but by being able to participate so fully in her manner of operation, I believed that my own way, whatever it was, was available to me also. What impressed me was her ability to move straight to the heart of the matter, to say what she saw and make no bones about it, even if the person resisted or did not fully understand. And through the poetic intensity of her answers she sent people directly back to themselves, to their own puzzlement and therefore to further questioning. They wanted pat answers, but she refused to cater to those kind of simplistic expectations, refused to let them escape from the more complex configurations of self-responsibility and its relationship to the truth. All this came across with a tone of loving ruthlessness, which to me announced a fierce commitment to stay with people when they were disturbed by their darkest fears. As teacher she was one in a million and I wanted more.

After that first encounter I hounded her for several weeks. It was not easy since she did not make herself readily available, but gradually, without either of us needing to define what was going on, I entered into informal training under her. This meant that I attended as many of her groups as I could and so put myself in the way of as much close attention as I needed. In the process, she slowly brought out the seer in me, understanding at the same time what I needed to do to release him. What I needed was actually very simple, although at the time it did not feel simple at all. In her words, I had to 'open my mouth'. She showed me how much I had been holding back, how much I had been seeing in people and not expressing. This was not because I had not wanted to, but because it was associated with a very deep-seated fear. I began to remember how crazy I had been made to feel for the vivid impressions that went through me as a child and how thoroughly I had censored the words before they could even rise to the back of my throat. I had lost my own language, lost trust that the way I needed to be with people so as to touch their innermost core was valid in any form. It was like learning to talk again, embarrassed as I was that a teacher of twenty-five years experience should have to halt and stutter in order to express what he had to say. I came to groups and sat in silence as she worked with someone, engrossed in the whole process and confirming, with a certain amount of self-satisfaction, my own perceptions as I went along. Then without warning, she would turn to me and say, "Well, come on then, speak." And I would instantly go blank. Everything I had tracked up to that very moment would vanish into thin air, leaving me blushing and stammering and hiding in shame. She laughed a lot and teased me lightly, but her belief in me never went away. She did not accept my paralysis as the real thing, and when I finally risked opening my mouth, she was right there with the encouragement that had never come my way as a child.

It was in this way that I became aware of the extent of the damage of my schooling years. That is in itself a long story, but let it simply be said that education at boarding schools in Scotland was hardly ideal encouragement for the intuitive imagination. And I soon found out that I was not the only one to suffer from such traditional forms of schooling, based as it was on the acquisition of knowledge and not in the least concerned with the development of perceptive powers or the skills of human communication. The education I had received, or not received, had clearly interfered with whatever intuitive sense had once been mine. I remembered arriving at school at seven years old, bursting with questions about everything under the sun and excelling through this enthusiasm to know all that there was to know. This lively curiosity lasted about a year until I found myself confronted by a new teacher who mocked my questions and sneered at all my answers. I stopped questioning for many years after that, always waiting in terror for the mockery that was bound to come my way as a matter of course. These memories became more intense as I continued this training, surfacing with great pain as, at the same time, my original fluency began to return. Memories returned also of a still earlier time when my curiosity was even more alive and deep contact with people my primary joy.

Then some other interferences began to make themselves known. By this time my mouth was opening more readily, to the extent of coming out with what seemed like bizarre pronouncements about the painful intricacies of people's lives. Alarmed by these sudden outpourings, I would stop myself in mid-stream certain that I would only be received with anger. I imagined this anger taking the form of incredulous disbelief, followed by accusations that I had no idea what I was talking about. When I realized that they actually wanted more, that I was being received with acceptance and appreciation, I was overwhelmed. I was moved emotionally in a way that I did not understand. It was as if their acceptance and welcome were mine also, confirmation that what I had been seeing and feeling was valid after all and not some gross blunder that was liable to turn me into a fool. With the confusion of these emotions a further memory returned. It was of a younger child, three or four years old, who felt that the whole sensory world was at his disposal. He had a very distinct language of feeling and spoke out, without hesitation, to put those feelings into words as best he knew how. It seems he was given full rein at first, then something threw him into confusion. What he said was all at once no longer welcomed, but received instead with anger even though he himself had not changed. This memory was not of any particular incident, but came to me on a feeling level, as if at that point something in my whole being had shifted, forcing me to adapt to pressures that were too strong to withstand. I gave up something, an original way of operating in the world that was more my own than anything I had replaced it with since. With this teaching I felt that I was recontacting the ease and openness of that earlier time, coming back into a mode of expression that had been lost to me for many years.

With all this an impression began to form of how many

children had hidden away the words they originally wanted to use because of the disturbed response of the adults surrounding them; how they must have then assumed a substitute language, a language created only to please. I began to understand how rarely children are allowed to be the truth-tellers they naturally are because they are born among people who need, for their survival, to hide away what is real about their lives. These children are born to perceive deeply and accurately what is going on around them, but the fear generated by the adults around them takes the truth of those perceptions away. When I touched again on the purity of my own small child, I uncovered a quality of intimacy that had long been denied me, a closeness of connection that had been my way of knowing that I really belonged. What I had been taught was most insane in me was actually my sanest commodity, because surely sanity is based on a belief that we can belong and have abilities to make contact with those we wish to know as kin.

To reclaim this intuitive sense after so long meant rediscovering a basic intimate connection with others. Although on a different level, it was not very different from what I had felt happening in those moments of spontaneous invention when teaching improvisational theater. While the flow was uninterrupted and the impulse pure, the actor took on a luminous presence that effortlessly drew the co-actors and the audience into a very intimate level of communication. When at his best, the actor literally bared the essence of his soul, setting no limits to the degree of intimacy that was possible. And now, with these new discoveries, I was beginning to see how this quality of intimacy could be equally available on a day-to-day basis, how it would begin to be accessible as soon as there was no need to edit or censor any information about a person that came through. It was like a short cut that went straight to the heart, eliminating all the other languages that had been imposed by the mind's ingenuity as substitutes for the truth. To move through to the other side of those substitute languages was to reclaim the power of close contact being to being. There was no more playing of roles, no more of the masks that had become a necessity as soon as the original bid for intimacy failed. It was remarkable to note how many circuitous routes of communication had been developed when it had originally been so simple. The short cut to the heart was the original, direct route, followed faithfully until fear of the truth forced it to close.

Something remarkable happens to a person when the truth is not dangerous anymore, when it can be spoken out clearly without fear. From that moment life begins again from a place that is real. A space opens up where there are no rules to follow or games to be played. It is what all children want from their earliest years: freedom to express in whatever way is theirs, with acceptance, without being blamed or ignored. It was this state I had returned to by the time this vital training was done. My mouth had finally opened, and I was finding out how to encourage others to do the same. The result, now that my original language was flowing more smoothly, was a glimpse of a grand conspiracy forming whereby all those who had been labeled as different or weird came together and simply recognized one another, accepted in each other the special language with which they were born.

•

IV. THE EMOTIONAL FLOW

The beginnings of my emotional recovery coincided, not surprisingly, with my initial forays into improvisational theater. I had to wait until I was thirty-five years old to discover that I was a deeply feeling person who had stored away in an unreachable reservoir every major emotional incident of his life. The moment when that reservoir was first tapped literally divided my life in two. The whole quality of my experience changed. The effect was so immediate that at the time I wondered whether I was going to be able to survive the transition. Even now, when I look back on those first thirty-five years, they seem strangely one dimensional, almost, at times, unreal. I remember quite clearly certain things that happened to me, some good and some bad, but I cannot get really close to them, cannot move inside. They are set in a single tone with little to distinguish between what affected me and what did not. I can only conclude that my emotional nature, like my intuitive sense, was reduced little by little so that life could be dealt with in a more manageable and efficient way. Both intuition and emotions interfered with that level of efficiency and so had to be eliminated as soon as possible. Without them I learned what was required of me, which was to move from one experience to another steadily and consistently, accepting whatever came my way without fuss. The first priority was for me to harness any untoward emotional outbursts so that they would not intrude on the image of happiness that had to be presented to the outside world. Expressions of joy or appreciation were allowed, but never anything like anger, fear, grief or despair. As the child became man, nagging voices pestered me occasionally, puzzled that there was not more to life and asking me if I were not missing something. But I soon became successful enough as the world saw it, so the voices never lasted very long. After all, I had been scrupulously trained to manage life without upset, so I was not about to let those kind of pessimistic voices get me down.

However, there was one time in my life, what I would call now my first year of attempting to be a man, when those voices became more insistent. In fact, they almost took me down, despite all my efforts to silence them. They entered my body in a physically violent take-over bid and, for a few terrifying months, refused to let go. I had no idea what was happening to me and was unable to tell anyone anything about it for fear that I would discover something to be seriously wrong. I was eighteen, under severe pressure from my first teaching job, and my mother had recently died. In retrospect I know that I was suffering from 'panic attacks' and the strain of everything I was going through was crying out for my feelings to join in. But I had lost contact with those emotional channels many years ago. I had forgotten how they could be of service to me and now they were combining forces in a massive revolt that could not any longer be controlled. During the worst moments I believed I was going insane and was, in fact, on the point of admitting my madness to the world when I fell in love for the first time. Then, as mysteriously and unpredictably as they had taken me over, those pent-up feelings pulled back and faded away. However the whole experience remained with me like a hideous warning, and there were several other times in the next few years when that monster threatened to devour me. Never for very long did he allow me to forget him. Internally he circled me in prolonged strategic maneuvers, teasing me with the cliff-edge of an experience that I was terrified to approach again. He also ensured that my emotions were kept even further at bay. The flat, level mode returned and my determination to stave off any upset became stronger still.

All this changed one dramatic afternoon during the final moments of a massage. The soothing nature of touch was relatively new to me then and for the first time my body was learning to relax and enjoy its pleasuring sensations. However, for me it was an experience of the body only; I was quite innocent as yet of the close connection between touch and the emotions. This one afternoon, the session was about over and the masseuse was finishing with soothing strokes up and down my spine. All at once my body leapt in uncontrollable spasms. It jerked around on the table as if it had, once and for all, decided to take on a life of its own. The masseuse kept contact with her hands and quite calmly asked me to stay with my body and just let its movements take me over. And take me over they did, the spasms continuing with an ever-increasing power and intensity. Then, forcing its way through from a faraway place inside, rising up in waves and desperate to find its way to the surface came a deep, sobbing cry, an unearthly sound that I could hardly believe was my own. The sobbing tore at my body and before long I was gasping for breath, unable to find enough air to support the energy that was rushing through. Clearly my whole system was making a mammoth effort to reverse the stifling process that had been going on for so long. I cried until my body was physically drained. All that remained was a profound weakness along with a new sensation of softness and pliability, unfamiliar to my body as I had previously known it. My emotions had finally found their passage, and session after session, they kept on coming through, a whole new language that refused to identify itself in anything like an orderly way. Overcome by this invasion, I was unable at first to link the feelings with any particular experience; for it was clear that my mind had been deliberately outlawed from the proceedings in order for my emotions to re-engage. Then more specific memories began to take shape, the first ones leading directly to my mother's death and the natural process of grieving that I had closed down. With the help of those memories, my emotional life slowly began to reassemble itself. I was finally able to grasp the enormity of what I had been missing and the importance of making up for lost time.

A massive backlog had built up and I felt the outpouring would never end. Relationships changed, sexual experience changed, and life became, for the first time since I had stowed all those emotions away, alarmingly unpredictable. Gone were the consistency and the reliability I had associated myself with so closely, qualities that I did not intend to give up gracefully by any means. For this emotional language loved playing havoc with things, and it was difficult for me to accept that the order of my life was no longer under control. I began to understand how freely expressive the first years of my childhood had been, and with this understanding came an urgent need to re-experience those years from the feeling child's point of view. The extent of the difference was hard to believe. From a closed emotional state my childhood appeared to be a happy existence, including a great deal of love and care. If I suspected at any time that someone may have behaved towards me in a hurtful manner, I was ready to spring to their defense and make up any number of excuses for their unseemly behavior. Yet, I was also aware of this state as somewhat elusive and cloudy. I kept losing track of my own identity and my true reactions to people and situations around me. But when I brought my newly activated emotions along with me, the picture changed. Instead of feeling cared for, I felt alone and unseen, continuously confused by how other people responded to me. I was so strikingly different from anyone else that I felt like a stranger, with no points of reference for my own strangeness. But as the emotions kept moving through, informing me of how much expression had been forbidden in my life, a strength and uniqueness emerged from within that stranger, giving me hints of a richness of spirit that might have thrived had there been more encouragement.

As soon as I was confident that my emotional life was here to stay, I turned my attention, with a teacher's fascination, to the means by which it had made its way to the surface again. What was it that had the power to reach down so far and bring back to life such a vital part of my experience? The simplest answer was the power of touch, and certainly to become aware of the importance of touch was an appropriate starting point for my research. I began to absorb the remarkable skills of my masseuse and identify what it was about her touch that drew out the secret stories my body contained. She worked on the principle that every point in the body was connected to an emotional center and that physical pressure was a means of speaking to the buried stress. I understood this on a technical level, yet sensed that technique only covered a small aspect of the whole. What seemed more important to me was the undivided attention which accompanied her touch so closely. It was a quality of attention that gave limitless space to the feelings that emerged. The completeness of her focus created a pure, open space for anything to happen, however raucous, however awkward, however bizarre. There was full permission given for me to release my full expressive range. No sense, no logic was required. Whatever sounds came through, they could ride with the waves of feeling and not worry about being closed down. I became a quiet child, but I discovered that there must have been a lot of noise at some point before the quiet was imposed. So the room we worked in became open territory, set up so that the imposed quiet could be broken apart again. It was a process of shattering, and the random sounds that came out of me reverberated through my body and contributed to a loosening of all the set patterns inside. At the center was this calm woman, acting as a catalyst for it all with a firm touch, a strong presence, and a minimum of explanations or words.

However, the qualities I admired in her continued to be somewhat of a mystery because they had nothing to do with the mind. The mind was really all I had known. I must have picked up at a very early age that, if my feelings were not going to stay around to support me, something else would have to take their place. I had to be protected somehow, and the mind was the only part that seemed to know how to manipulate and rearrange the truth. It became suddenly obvious why I had moved so directly from the emotionless atmosphere of my schools and family into a series of academic institutions. The intellectual life did not come easily to me or even house me very comfortably once I had taken it on. In fact, at an early stage of my undergraduate studies, I rejected both theater and music as possible subjects for specialization. They were my most passionate concerns, but too close to the heart for comfort, too frightening to commit myself to wholesale. So eventually I chose to keep a safe distance from them in order to avoid the risk of their powerful emotional pull. I made certain that my intellect would be the one to take care of me and keep me for as long as possible from the contacts in which my feelings were too strong. I also began to understand why a more traditional, verbal form of therapy had never come my way. Any approach based on words, on dialogue, would have been doomed to failure in the face of all the mental gyrations I had developed in my own defense. I would only have been reminded of the distance that had existed for so long between myself and other people, the barriers of abstract words which had always kept me from what I loved most. As I considered this, I became increasingly aware of how far the mind could separate from the emotions and how limited words were as a means of healing the rift. The function they so often took on was to impose an emergency order on the emotions' natural disorder, forcing confinement on what needed to run wild.

But it was certainly a surprise to find that emotions, once their wildness was returned to them, took on an order of their own. Once the floodgates opened, I more or less resigned myself to the fact that my life would never come to order again. The upheavals kept coming and my mind kept trying to resist the inevitable chaos that ensued. Yet all the time, unknown to me, another order was forming; not one that I could control or leave my mark on, but an order nonetheless. It was a natural order that took time to establish, one that was not forced on the system in any way, but, at certain unexpected moments, let me know it was there. Its identity made itself known through the rhythm of daily life, through a way events had of developing their own natural sequence when I least expected it. Any order I planned in advance began to fall apart, while underneath a different rhythm made itself known, if I allowed it to, and if I was prepared to abandon the original design. As I caught onto the changes, I was reminded of the natural rhythms that would spring out of nowhere during theatrical improvisations, moments when an immediate impulse would insist that the body's imagination take over. For this to happen the mind had to move completely out of the way; otherwise its emergency function as protector would take over, imposing a form in advance that had nothing to do with the body's spontaneous desires.

All the time this personal process was going on, I was continuing to teach theater. I was also studying massage and adapting it to my work with improvisation. It was part of the sensory language that I developed at that time and was particularly effective in dealing with physical tightness and strain. But despite my own personal changes, as teacher these emotional aspects stayed out of range. Towards the end I was beginning to recognize when emotional blockages in the students interfered with the creative process, but the environment was not conducive to further development in that area. This was one of the reasons why I was compelled to leave. My own recent emotional release gave me to realize a striking absence of feeling within my theater work. The gap was becoming too wide between my role as teacher and my experience as a feeling man and it was becoming harder all the time to believe that a viable connection existed between them. So I cast off the role of theater teacher without even considering that I might return to it some day. It was true that I did return after a long period of rest and a radical change of location, but I entered in again from a very different angle, so different that I could scarcely connect it with my previous profession.

My re-entry came about like this. I was asked one day out of the blue to address a group on the subject of 'voice'. It was a subject I had taught for many years as part of actor's training, one that had interested me a great deal both inside the context of theater and outside of it. But I had never really had time to explore the outside context, which was to do with the subtlety of voice tones and how people give valuable information about themselves by the way they speak. During my work with actors I had thought about this aspect a great deal but never given it any public exploration. So I accepted the invitation and began the day by talking for a while about the different emotional moods a voice can express and how they can convey much about a person's history. I then selected certain members of the group as illustrations of the points I was making, asking them to speak and commenting on how their voices sounded. I was not very far along when, to my surprise, several people began to cry. I was somewhat unsettled by their reactions, but decided to continue and let the feelings run their course. The emotional tenor in the room continued to intensify, so I finally decided to take a break and see if things would settle down. After the break I led a series of vocal exercises to see if the energy could be absorbed in that direction, but the emotional atmosphere still persisted, leaving me with even less understanding of what was going on than before. The confusion of this day was to be my initiation into a whole new phase of teaching, although it took the experience of more groups to get a firmer grasp of the whole thing, to catch onto the fact that the emotional channels I had been clearing for myself were now opening and becoming available to others for the first time. And it was clear that, when those channels were open, form and subject-matter had little bearing on the matter; the emotions came through anyway. Which left me with my next challenge: how to support these people when their feelings were exposed, and then how to help connect them to what they were feeling.

I learned how to do this gradually as more experience came my way, taken aback by the range of emotion that kept coming through and by the immediate changes in people once they found permission to express themselves fully. In the process, I discovered a way to close the gap between my life and teaching, to draw out the hidden energy in myself and others simultaneously without restriction of form or anticipation of result. I could look forward to meeting with groups or individuals without any advance agenda, free to discover the full depth and range of human expression; free to work out the essential ingredients of support needed if the expression was going to take on its true nature without fear.

PART TWO. SUPPORTING

V. SAFETY

The first of those ingredients was undoubtedly safety. I had long been aware of the crucial part it played in any process of opening or change and had watched it ebb and flow in all my work with improvisation. At that time it was an element I could not control. I could only be a curious witness to its comings and goings. Some people exhibited extreme degrees of unsafety, while others were willing to go on risking no matter how much danger was involved. In one sense I took much of the risk-taking for granted, accepting it as a natural human desire to break new ground; although, in retrospect, I can see that the danger level was abnormally high and that there was something about the atmosphere I created that allowed for unusual feats to be performed. But there were always a few in each group who spent most of their time in extreme fear and were unable to break the paralysis that constrained them. These people I hardly got to know at all. They learned to become invisible very quickly, and I did not know how to lure them out of hiding.

But after the emotional out-break of the group I just described, the word 'safety' began to crop up all the time. When I was given feedback, the first point usually mentioned was the degree of safety in the room and what a difference it made. I got the impression that for many people this quality had been **the** missing element for a long time and now that it was finally offered, emotional waves were impossible to control. I took the feedback seriously and began an equally serious inquiry into the whole phenomenon, simply because it appeared to be an essential foundation for this new phase of my teaching. From the outset I knew that it had something to do with my own presence because there was no method or technique through which I brought this safety into conscious operation. It was not something I could conjure up upon request; it was simply there as an integral part of what I was doing. I also knew this quality was connected to the ease I felt within myself in the face of extreme emotional expression, the fact that I was not uncomfortable, but rather welcomed the outpouring as my masseuse had for me. I also found that the safety did not disappear when I expressed my own feelings within the group; if anything, the safety level seemed to increase, presumably because they recognized my kinship with their own experiences. From this I deduced that it was mainly what was hidden that brought on sensations of unsafety; the fears dissolved simply because they had a chance to come out of hiding. These were obvious truths that I could catch onto right away, but out of them arose far more complex issues.

In some situations the function of safety was easy to understand; for example, when the feelings connected to some sudden shock of childhood, the kind of shock that put an end to the possibility of trusting and left behind a haunting expectation of further interference in the future. In these cases the safety enabled a return to those moments of pain under more accepting conditions. Through a full expression of the feelings involved, the pain could be released that in its buried state had exercised much power over their adult lives. But there were others whose shock moments were not so easy to identify. There was a particularly stark quality of terror in certain people that I could not place, as if they had never experienced even a beginning of safety on which to build their lives. The fear did not seem to be related to specific events of childhood, but was more pervasive, embedded, it seemed, within the very structure of the cells. It expressed itself in the form of a hyper-fragility that appeared to have nothing substantial underneath it at all. It took me a while to realize that it was a baby's fragility I was dealing with and an issue of safety that needed to be traced back to birth. There was one striking characteristic that belonged to people of this kind: they identified instantly with any unexpressed feelings in the room, to such a degree that they would lose touch completely with their own identity. They literally abandoned themselves and fused with the individuals in distress. I discovered they had no control over this sudden shift and were, for the most part, unaware of the change. They were also confused by the muddle that ensued when we tried to sort out whose feelings belonged to whom.

At first I found these identity-switching tactics hard to believe, but they happened again and again, forcing me to look very closely at the distortions possible in a baby's experience. I considered what it would be like if a baby, with its subtle sensitive nature still intact, responded not to the surface behavior, but to the hidden emotional states of those who took on the parental role. I imagined that the baby would respond with alarm to this inner turmoil and, in a kind of emergency panic, go searching for some form of protection for itself. In the baby's newborn vulnerable condition there would be little opportunity for relaxation, so somewhere along the lines an escape route would have to be worked out, or at least a way of relieving some of the anxiety provoked by those unexpressed emotions. Certainly to merge with them would be preferable to being at their mercy; preferable to this crazy mix-up of emotions and the unnatural division between the inside and the outside. The surface behavior might indicate some semblance of caring, but what if the repressed feelings contradicted this outward show of support? What if the attention was only skin deep? The impulse would then be to close the gap, to bring what was hidden to the surface so that it didn't leap out unexpectedly and do the baby harm. In those conditions the least safe place would be the baby's own body and to move inside one of the caretakers would at least offer a better chance of protection.

The likely result of all this would be a hyper-alert state of consciousness, one that travelled with lightning speed from person to person in a frantic effort to avoid pain and make sense out of such incomprehensible behavior. I imagined it to be a brilliant strategy for survival, but one that took a terrible toll because, before long, all possibility for relaxation would be gone. The child's consciousness would develop a perpetually scanning radar screen always on the alert for approaching danger. An inevitable equation surrounds this exhausting procedure, one that would develop more subtlety and refinement as the child grew older: the quicker the merge with another person, the less likely the possibility of pain.

This hypothesis became more and more real to me over the years. Now I am quick to recognize those people who come in the door, put one step over the threshold, and frantically scan with their radar system to track down the smallest evidence of hidden feelings lurking in the the room. If they find that evidence, they are gone already, leaping out of themselves to monitor the situation, not allowing a single suspicion to go unexplored. If, however, they find no evidence, the first reaction is usually a bewilderment of disbelief, followed by overwhelming relief when they realize they can finally return to themselves and allow whatever is there to begin its own course of unfolding. It is a remarkable experience to witness that initial return after such a long absence. The body does not quite know what to do with it, evacuated as it has been for so long by any kind of independence or repose. Often it will go into spasms of resistance and conflict, taken over by the sheer quantity of energy wanting to come through. In this case what safety represents is space to move around in, both physical and psychic. It means the possibility of operating without other people becoming obstacles to negotiate or objects of scrutiny and suspicion. But before this freedom of movement can be recovered, the baby's state of confusion has to be fully felt, the physical helplessness of having no soothing sensitivity at hand. The body's expression of this confusion can be fierce, re-enacting as it does the original shock at life's confusion, the appalling recognition of life as an erratic and hazardous undertaking.

It is hard to convey how highly developed this radar system becomes when safety is threatened that early. It is also infallibly accurate, as I have been shown to my discomfort again and again. It is accurate despite the fact that it has no sense of proportion;

meaning that it will not pick up the safe elements to balance the unsafe, but will home in ruthlessly on the danger only, exaggerating all that is unsafe in any person within range. I soon learned that when this kind of extreme scrutiny is being exercised, an uncompromising openness is required of me, a willingness to acknowledge things about myself that I may not even be in touch with at the time. People with this baby-shock experience are truthtellers and have been trained in this skill through the unending strain of survival. So unless I remain open and acknowledge the validity of what they perceive, any safety that has already been established will immediately close down. Creating this safety depends on a wholehearted willingness to enter the other's territory and find out what it has to offer, no matter how bizarre it may appear from the outside. It is a matter of following the other's lead, allowing the person to reveal the landscape in all its detail. An unsafe life creates a bizarre landscape, one that does not rest on much that is rational or orderly. And its intricacies and details will only be shown to someone who is willing, from the outset, to believe and accept rather than object and contradict the information provided. Besides, the inside tour of this landscape is the only release. These unsafe people have only their own versions of reality to go on and it is often the case that, after many years of misunderstanding and denial from others, they begin to doubt that it is real themselves. They stop believing that the extremes of their own life really happened and have to be fully joined in their experience for it to take on true substance again.

So if any change is to take place, I have to sustain deep levels of safety through a tempestuous and disorderly journey. In the process, because my good faith is under constant suspicion, I have to establish myself as a fallible, feeling co-traveller who is ready to reveal his own limitations and the genuine nature of his responses. Throughout the journey the quality of this safety will be constantly tested, whether consciously or unconsciously, to ensure that I am present and I am real; and by real I mean a fellow human being who does not hide fears and doubts of his own. If there are fears, they have to come out into the open immediately, because it was the hidden element that brought on the danger in the first place and created the original confusion.

Once the element of trust is thoroughly established and has been challenged again and again, there is a quite miraculous turnaround, a paradoxical shift that lies at the heart of the whole process. The thrill of risk and danger becomes available again. By offering support through to the other side of fear, the excitement of the unknown can be welcomed back and connected to the child's naturally given spirit of adventure. Children whose security is threatened early spend whole lives obsessed with safety, obsessed with a need to protect themselves and with the fear that they will never adequately be able to do so. This concern preempts any potential for meeting life in an open and embracing way. The safety they are hell-bent on providing for themselves in their emergency situation is all-consuming and completely swamps the spirit of curiosity, that energetic zest for all the wonders and details of the world they have been born into. Risk is a basic, natural impulse; it creates the impetus to reach beyond what is within immediate range. So within the frame of safety the power of risk can be recovered again, the challenge of danger once more welcomed in. This has nothing to do with the danger created by unstable, fearful parents and their unreasonable demands; rather it is the danger involved in exploring new environments and discovering whatever powers of self-expression lie waiting to be unfurled. On this level the next unknown is always there to be challenged. Excitement rises to the surface and adrenaline courses through the veins. But there is no opportunity for this version of fear to even begin to find its flow until the struggle for survival has been laid low and a core of safety drawn from deep inside. Then the being can be touched gently again and reminded of the powers of invention that are waiting to be found.

So the value of safety is that it offers a full spiral of release. The first stage of that release is activated by a belief that safety does, after all, exist. In other words, there is nobody in the vicinity who threatens unpredictable behavior or who needs to be taken care of. Extreme measures of protection are not required. This foundation allows for a spiral downward into the depth of insecurity experienced by the child, a surrender to the physical and emotional upheavals that could not be handled at the time. Then comes the gradual, uneasy turning-point during which the possibility of risk is awakened again, a fresh curiosity coming alive and drawing with it a new quality of energy from inside. Rather than being invaded by the outside world on someone else's terms, the being finds support to go out and meet life's excitement on its own terms. Through safety unsafety becomes accessible once more because the element of risk is re-aligned with a sense of adventure rather than with a feeling of helplessness and doom. There is a fear that brings on paralysis, associated with overwhelm from insensitive people; and there is the fear that arises naturally in the process of breaking new ground. The first is a fear that is diminishing, unsupported and closed; the second has support underneath it, space around it and a potential for unlimited expansion. So it is the changing face of fear that facilitates the upward turn of the spiral, that puts into motion the desire to move up and out again. It is also at this point that the spark of creativity catches fire and spontaneity is given an opportunity to come alive again.

Once these foundations are established, the presence of safety ceases to become such a large priority. What at the beginning of the process manifested as extreme dependence now transforms into the naturally fierce independence of a child who is determined to do everything on its own. The rhythm of recovery varies with each individual: one person can be given safety for a single day and the whole world changes, while another will need to move through the spiral inch by inch over a period of months or years. Whatever the timing, however long it takes for the safety to recreate foundations of strength, there is always a tenacious quality of independence that emerges. Besides, another natural impulse has, by this time, found recovery: the impulse to reach out and find support in times of need. In the original state of unsafety this impulse is forced into reverse so that pushing away becomes the automatic gesture, showing how much despair has accumulated at ever making contact again. So to offer safety, to simply stay around through all the doubts and fears of rejection, is to give back the impulse to reach out to others, is to restore faith in the fact that support from others can be found. If belief in one person can be thoroughly established, then others will be found also, and chosen wisely. Belief in support is the final piece in the recovered state of independence and self-safety; belief in one's own reality as foundation, backed by the option to connect with the inspiration of others when the need arises. When both are available, a natural free-wheeling autonomy becomes possible again.

VI. PRESENCE

When I worked with actors, I found out that presence was the single most difficult quality to find. Yet without it everything else that they attempted was hollow and untrue. Year after year we searched it out like a precious jewel, and the more we searched, the more essential it became. For example, there were some students who came in with exaggerated pretensions of grandeur, believing that the more they gesticulated and flailed around, the more the audience would pay attention to them. Even when they were asked to sit in a chair alone in the middle of the stage and do nothing, at the slightest provocation head, face, arms, and finally the whole body would spasmodically rebel against this required stillness. As often as not they would be quite unaware of these automatic movements, and when I pointed them out or even physically restrained them, they became overwhelmed by debilitating feelings of impotence. Then there were those of an opposite tendency whose inhibitions prevented them from making large of anything; yet this exercise in stillness was equally impossible for them also. Give them central stage focus without movement and all they expressed was a desperate need to disappear from sight, a shrinkage of all those attributes that could have been considered strong. It was remarkable to observe how something that seemed so simple became such a challenging ordeal. In time I discovered that these opposite reactions to the same situation were not opposites at all. Whether there was a compulsion to move or a desperation to disappear, both clearly stemmed from an inability to accept that the being, unmoving and unadorned, could transmit any semblance of power. They had no faith that their simple presence could draw attention towards them or that anything significant could possibly be going on while they waited, without action, word or facial expression, for the audience to engage. They had no idea that quiet and stillness, rather than inducing boredom, could titillate expectation, could contain its own charge of intensity in making out of the smallest gestures something potentially very large.

This was certainly not favorable testimony to the amount of acknowledgement they had been given in their lives. I could only conclude that little space had been allowed them in their lives to be their most natural selves. The awkwardness and embarrassment under such simple exposure were obviously not born within them, so what influence had been brought to bear to make them that way? Where was that original confident stand that must have existed at some point in time? I was confronted either with unnatural substitutions that had something to do with needing approval, or attempts at self-elimination which meant that someone else had tried to do the eliminating before they had. Either way the original confidence, which must have asserted itself at some time with natural pride, was scarcely to be seen. Gone was the freedom to do or not do according to their own will and gone also was a trust that they would be able to attract others without emergency energy or devious means. An inherent simplicity had been taken away. And obviously theater was not the only place to be suffering from these distortions. The context of performance and the anticipation of an audience certainly made this kind of exposure more searing and unavoidable, but there was no way that life itself was going to be exempt from the desperation and artificiality of such poses. In this aspect, I began to recognize that there was not much difference between theater and life. In fact, it was my involvement in theater that drew me into a closer observation of life, a closer awareness of the masquerades that were daily played out before me, substitutes for a simple presence which had never been acknowledged as enough or worthwhile.

In this context I became particularly curious about certain actors I was working with who only needed to step into a performing area for all attention to be drawn towards them. Even if there was considerable action circulating in the area around them, their presence continued to command the stage. They carried with them a natural fullness and relaxation, a deliberation of movement and expression that had a precise rhythm all its own. No effort was wasted, nothing thrown away. It was the economy of gesture that seemed to draw attention most of all. I realized that this was equally true off-stage, that this same sense of presence could be established simply by a person entering a room. The same principles applied. In any contact, whether on or off stage, there were those who attracted a lot of attention around them without effort, and there were those who tried all the tricks in the book, who expended a great deal of energy, without anything like the same results. There might be a surface entertainment value that caught people in a momentary aura of dazzle, but even so the attention was still likely to be reluctant and short-lived. The effortless presence, however, invited attention without manipulating it in any way, and it seemed to be the freedom of space that gave it its deeper quality. There was no pressure, but open invitation to let the developing relationship take its natural course. I sensed that I was witnessing the very beginnings of intimacy where giving and receiving met on equal terms to celebrate the unpressured space around them. Whether it was an actor/audience relationship or an everyday personal exchange, a fluidity of communication became possible that encouraged the masks to fall and invited in what was of value behind them.

From there I was able to imagine for the first time a child's ideal environment. Given this kind of spacious invitation, a child would have no need for substitute forms of expression, no need to search desperately for whichever form of behavior would guarantee the most attention. Furthermore, there would be no embarrassment associated with any natural state of being, whether that state be silent or loud, still or wildly dancing; for there would be nothing to set off the process of adaptation, no catalyst for those ingenious methods of play-acting or hiding. It was a while before I was able to recognize how much sensitivity and beauty lay underneath those disguises and how much people wanted to be free of them. Only when my own intuitive senses returned was I able to understand the extent of the fears involved and the subtle shadings of protection. But once that understanding came in, I was able to assist people in those first tentative steps towards freedom and assure them that they would be given an open space to make them. Once the fear of judgment was released, the effect was instantaneous: those who had wanted to disappear found a light in their eyes, a jauntiness in their gait and a desire to inhabit their physical bodies totally for the first time. While those who had felt compelled to perform found a resting place through which they could accept themselves as real without strain.

The actor who affects an audience most deeply is the one who takes on a chosen role without reservation. The more the role is embraced, the fuller the aliveness on stage. Likewise, in day-to-day life, the person who affects us deeply is the one who inhabits all of the self without reservation. The power of an individual who is wholly present is entirely self-generating in that it has thrown off the need for any form of adaptation as a pleasing mechanism for others.

So, if offering safety is the first ingredient for support, presence does not come far behind. It acts as an essential catalyst for the unmasking to begin. Just as teaching theater is preparation for the moment when the actor, with the fullest presence possible, comes face to face before an audience; so to be with someone in a supportive environment is preparation for that individual to engage more fully in life. It is essential for both theater and life to have an arena of experimentation, an environment in which certain risky ways of being can be tested before being exposed to the larger challenge of an audience or the outside world. And for this to be effective, there must be full participation, a joint exploration through which these new ways of being can be given all possible variations. This joint exploration must have, as a first requirement, an open, neutral space, fully available to an incoming person as clear ground. As co-explorer this does not mean that I absent myself in any way. It means that it is the other person's ground first of all, while I remain present and alert and still to support the other's journey in whatever direction it needs to go, which is not very different from the full, waiting presence of an actor around which the events of a drama are about to unfold. Although in this case it is not the unfolding of an already prepared script, but pure improvisation from the moment the other person enters the room and leads the way into what we are about to explore. I am there to offer the ideal setting: myself fully present and an open space for the full range of life to unfold. The more I am present, without judgment or expectation of what is to come, the quicker the other will be prepared to make the first move and lead the way.

If this kind of scenario is established at the very beginning, it brings with it a very special quality of invitation. There is safety in my presence, and there is also a heightened level of perception brought on by a guarantee of unlimited attention without interruption, a guarantee that the focus will not suddenly change. The room becomes a center for undivided attention, fulfilling a basic need in every individual, no matter how uncomfortable it may at first feel for those who have been starved of it all their lives. It is quality attention from someone entirely present, 'quality' being the key word. It is remarkable how many people there are who believe they had sufficient attention as a child and are puzzled as to why, as adults, they keep on yearning for more. They yearn for it because what they believed was attention was not actually attention at all; it was a semblance of physical presence deprived of focus and genuine interest, a distracted kind of hovering around that leaves the child in a state of constant frustrated desire. For those who only received that kind of attention full presence has an immediately liberating effect. A long-time nagging need disappears, giving rise to many new levels of feeling; not to speak of the rediscovery of their own capacity for presence, their chance now to slough off all the unnatural dramatic gestures they have taken on as a means of getting the attention that always eluded them.

So the essential dynamic that develops is of one fully present individual drawing out the latent presence of another. What happens underneath as this evolves is a restoration of faith that open territory exists, and that meetings can take place without pressure or confinement of any kind. The two people are simply there. There is no energetic intrusion, no imposition of belief structures or unnatural rhythms; and there is no danger of being stranded, no digressions into other streams of concern that do not belong to the meeting at hand. The respect shown to someone fully present is the means of absorbing a new quality of energy, one drawn instinctively into the innermost cells. The effect is profound, offering something that the child has always anticipated as a natural right and now gathers to itself in immediate recognition. At a theatrical performance, when I am invited to be fully present in the world evoked by the actors and when they are fully present for me, there is a quality of meeting that touches me deeply. Equally powerful is the release when the same quality of presence is available for a person's life experience, as if a sacred meeting ground has already been prepared and all that is needed is a mutual agreement to participate to whatever depth is required.

In this way a foundation is established from which to launch in any direction. It is also a place to return to from whatever flight of discovery is undertaken. It acts as a grounding for the whole procedure and a still center through which all excess and complications are swept away. Sometimes there is a reluctance to return because, by doing so, that naked, vulnerable form of being is again without disguise, and cannot resume those tricks of habit that have become so familiar. Yet it **is** important to keep returning because, whatever the direction of the journey, the old and the new are likely to become confused, the imposed behavior returning as interference to more recently discovered responses. It is a process of reeling out and reeling in again, making sure that there is the clear ground of presence for both people to find strong and equal footing on, a place of mutual recognition and a reminder of the simple, uncluttered attention that is available. It is the belief in this last that wavers most, particularly in moments of sudden, fearful realizations; and its reliability will have to be tested repeatedly before automatic impulses of protective behavior completely subside.

In the final effect presence is the most uncomplicated form of alliance. It is the clearest way to establish that manipulation does not have to be a part of relationships. If I look back on my own lonely childhood, my longing to ease that loneliness appears in the form of someone who comes and sits quietly beside me without saying a word; someone who simply wants to be there, no matter what my state of being; someone who does not inquire too closely into the causes of my condition, yet shows no indication of wanting to go away. I often used to wonder why this loneliness was not eased by busy social affairs and the fun and games that were a large part of my family life. Only later did I realize what a forced atmosphere that was for me, despite the fact that I had the capacity to adapt to its loudness and laughter. In my happiness I was acceptable, as long as the fervor of action and involvement continued; but I knew that in the quieter times, in the unidentifiable moments when I was just me, nobody would want to be there. Nobody would be interested in the undemonstrative, small-feeling child who found such difficulty in expressing who he really was inside. That revelation might take a long time, might require someone to be there, possibly, for months or years. My yearning was for someone who would be available to me on a long-term basis without my having to feel ashamed of the unpredictable flux of my own moods. Then perhaps I would find out more about those moods myself and trust that they had some larger, more positive significance. The presence of another, as I was growing up, always meant that I had to be aware of and adapt to what the other person needed from me; and so presence became an enemy rather than a friend, aggravation rather than repose. It was a new experience for me to learn, many years later, that a person could be with me without exerting some form of pressure on me. It was also new, even later, to learn that a person could be altogether with me without the need for words as an overt form of communication. This last experience was a revelation indeed, and I understood then how much I had underestimated the power of human contact and how so much of what I had been shown as contact was merely a babble of voices in the wind.

VII. VOICE

I first became familiar with the complexity of voice dynamics through my work in the theater. It was a core aspect of actor training and as a teacher I took great pleasure in playing with all the varied possibilities it presented to me. I began by working with external techniques, teaching traditional concepts of voice such as powers of projection, clarity of diction, and tone control. But over the years I became increasingly interested in the more sensory qualities of sound, the range of expression the natural voice was capable of, yet seldom put to use in any lively way.

To explore this aspect more extensively, I experimented with extremes of vocal pitch and tone, developing exercises that helped to stimulate vibration in the different chambers of the body. For example, I showed how the highest pitch of sound—falsetto for men—vibrated from the bone cavities of the face and head, while the lowest pitch vibrated from the belly. With the use of certain vowel and consonant combinations I encouraged the students to locate these specific areas of resonance and play with the new quality of sounds that came from them. In this way the voice became an instrument of fun rather than a vehicle for speeches delivered effectively from the stage. And the more I emphasized the sound aspect, the quicker the voices changed, monotonous drones transforming into the freedom of musical improvisation. Those who were at first inhibited found themselves pleasantly surprised at what came out of their own mouths, and finally took great delight in making as much noise as they wanted, regardless of how it sounded. When the voice changed, other changes happened also that were harder to identify, as if some of the students were projected onto a precarious emotional edge by producing such an unusual range of sound. This energy added considerable force to the improvisational performances as well.

Sound was easier to play around with than words. It introduced a private language that could be formed on the instant without need for mutual understanding. So during the high risk of these performances sound was often the most powerful element, and with a closely integrated group of actors, vocal fireworks could explode out of nowhere, acting as stimulus for episodes that were the most imaginative and lively of all.

This aspect of my teaching stayed with me in a lasting way, which was why I choose the topic of 'voice' as my means of re-entry into the teaching world. I knew there was something about it that I had left unexplored and I was determined to examine it more closely. So for a while I set myself up as a specialist in voice, not this time wanting to attract performers or theater people, but hoping to draw those who, in whatever profession they had chosen, were not using their voice to the fullest extent of its range. What I soon discovered was that most people had lost the identity of their true voice. They had lost touch with how their original voice sounded and developed a substitute voice to replace the real thing. It seemed that they had been compelled to alter how they sounded so as to be more readily received by the outside world, leading me to wonder what situation in life had brought about such an undesirable change. It seemed strangely unproductive for the voice to have been funneled into such a limited range of expression when at one time it had a much richer tone. I applied some of the same techniques I had used with my theater students, exercises to help re-open the tonal range; but this time I focused not on the art of performance, but on making contact with the original voice that was hiding under the false overlay. It was a matter of entering a wedge between the original and the imposed voice so that the person was able to hear the difference, was able to hear how the one had become separated from the other. In the process I discovered that the act of self-listening was not easy for most people. At some point they had lost contact with the desire, or even the ability, to take pleasure in their own capacity for colorful sound. So the challenge was to reintroduce an old friend and ally, potentially lively and interesting, who had become mistaken for an old boor. This boor had already been assigned to some dreary automatic function and was clearly considered unworthy of any greater prestige.

By changing focus from theatrical performance to life experience, I was again touching on a disturbing emotional history that raised all sorts of delicate questions. Why, for example, had a perfectly good voice been abandoned so as to imitate the tones and inflections of someone else? Why did a naturally deep-voiced powerful woman insist on holding on to the pleading whine of a little girl? Why had this man developed a cruel, hard edge to his voice when his eyes registered a soft, gentle concern? And what about the lazy voice of a woman who almost put me to sleep when she was sitting down, but flashed fire as soon as she started moving around? To encourage people such as these to become more intimate with, even to enjoy again, the soundings of their own voices turned out to be a more complex and emotional process than I had imagined. For the more I entered a wedge between original and imposed voice, the more clearly a repetitive resistance emerged that took on marked similarities to the fearful defenses of a child; and behind this defensiveness, I knew, lay the cause of such an unnatural change. Each time I found my way through a gap in the defenses, there emerged some startling new quality of sound and along with it a strong emotional fear that informed me of how much had been forbidden, how much the child had been forced to fit into patterns of speech that others had imposed. Again my thoughts returned to the baby and how acute the aural sensitivity must have been at birth, intensifying the confusion and the pain.

Voice was, in effect, my first opening into the heightened sensitivity of sensation during infancy, leading me to understand how deeply a certain tone of voice could penetrate and leave a life-long mark. I found out that the ear was indeed the first sensory organ to develop in embryo, and at birth became the forerunner in receiving information. It was particularly susceptible to harsh sounds and the more subtle double meanings that all voices contain. If the parent voices had already adapted in their own way and were being used to mask feelings they did not want to show, the tonal messages given out would be inevitably confusing to the child. For example, there might be a great deal of love locked inside that could not find its way through to the vocal tone; or, conversely, there might be an imitation of loving tones imposed on the voice, masking a deep fear and resentment inside. Whatever the combination, the child would not hear a matching of feeling and tone and from that confusion would begin the wariness of not knowing whose reality to trust. Already the baby's reality would be unsettled by the ambiguity of the surrounding tone, uncertain as to where the original truth lay.

When I was quite small I learned to lie brilliantly. I had such a reputation that my mother invented tortuous schemes to catch me and expose me for the culprit she took me to be. Even when I was not at fault, she was ruthless in her campaign, which shows me how strongly I was identified as criminal and how important it must have been for me to develop increasingly skillful tactics of evasion. The confusion between truth and falsehood continued to haunt me throughout my childhood and I look back on it now as a web of misery that had already ensnared me before I was even aware of what was going on. It has taken me a long time to come to terms with the distortions that were involved then, but I do know now that my own sense of reality was completely swept from under me, leaving me with no foundations for self-belief. It was not until I began to focus on the influence of voice tones at that early age that the mystery of it began to clear. Most puzzling had been the source of it all. I did not know how it began or why I should have ever felt the need to lie. But if I was confused by the voices around me from the very beginning, by their mixed messages and contradictions, I would have surely had to adapt in some way to the game that was being played out before me. I would have had to enter the world of subterfuge and hidden inflections and try to outplay those who had already established the rules. I cannot see, otherwise, that there would have been any point in getting myself so entangled, because I must have known that my life would not be enhanced thereby. If I had had other options, I surely would not have chosen falsehood as a productive method of relating to people, particularly when they already had the advantage of physical size. Only after I understood the distortions of my own experience was I able to appreciate the power of directness and simple honesty, the relief felt by people when they could finally trust that there would be no lies. I also understood why more fear was provoked by what was said indirectly than by what was said directly and how the truth of people's lives could only come clear if all the ambiguities of tone were ruthlessly exposed.

A safe, supportive environment, then, has to bring with it a voice aligned directly with the truth, a clarity of tone that cuts through the web of ambivalence woven by those early voices and helps form a new foundation on which trust can be established. For when there is true tone, when the vibration of the voice and the intention behind it match one another, then there is an instant alignment of energy. Heart-to-heart communication becomes possible again.

Vocal tone has a strong influence on all forms of interaction. With its subtle range of variation it is an integral part of communication, no matter what degree of intimacy is involved. Even if I talk to someone in a simple, casual manner, the tone of my voice can throw that person back to a deeply engrained memory of the past. It can be a memory of harsh intrusion or it can be a memory of gentle, soothing sounds lost in the earliest years of childhood. If this is the case, before the words have even a chance to enter in, they are altered. They change tone mid-passage to become the words of someone else and my own identity partly disappears in the process. The conversation then takes on a different dimension. If the voice memory is harsh, the communication of the moment is likely to be difficult; if it is gentle, then an unexpected contact may be found, allowing the words to enter in more deeply than they otherwise would have done. What is more, the tone can undergo this kind of shift before the words have even begun. Silence is a prelude that has many tones and can provoke a wide range of reactions. Some people are terrified of it and some welcome it as if it were the dearest of friends. For some it brings back memories of unbearable tension, of a home atmosphere, for example, in which the parents never spoke to one another and held onto all feelings of anger and pain. No intimacy of contact was possible as long as the silence continued because it was so deeply connected to the fear of that anger on the point of exploding. But for others who have been surrounded for years by constant bickering the silence is a relief, a resting place in which there is finally peace and quiet. In both cases there is never an experience of auditory openness. Whether the child's energy is expended to ward off intrusion or the dread of violence erupting, a natural rhythm of expression is never allowed to evolve. The sound of the human voice, intended as a source of ease and comfort, becomes instead a source of alarm, distrust, and misunderstanding.

The recovery of silence is as vital as the recovery of stillness. Within it is couched the possibility for uninhibited sound to be born again. If from birth the open space is crowded out by the unwelcome sounds of others or if it is charged with an unspoken tension, there is no opportunity for the auditory impulses to develop in an organic way. What happens to replace this organic process is a protective impulse that involves either an interruption of the natural rhythms or a process of closing down. I have come across people who were told that, as babies, they cried endlessly for several months and then appeared to settle down. There is disturbing information in this admission, and I immediately suspect that much of that initial bawling was sheer protest against the inexplicable vibrations around them, ending in exhaustion and eventual resignation to overwhelming forces. I also suspect that much of the original sensory awareness closed down in the process and there was an immediate shift from a simplicity of receiving to some more deadened alternative. A shield was mounted against the grosser vibrations, an equivalent of ear plugs to safeguard the inner delicacy of the baby's hearing.

So the possibility of silence has to be re-established before the senses can begin to soften again, let down their guard. It has to be identified as neutral ground so that the original true tone can be tapped again. Through all the layers of mixed messages with which the human language has become associated, the ring of truth, the voice as nurturer, has to be heard again. It is like a lost language brought back into fluency again, a language in which the heart acts as the primary mediator. As the voice loses its original identity and takes on its various forms of disguise, there is, quite literally, a shift of foundation from the heart to the head. The heart closes down and the mind begins to work overtime. On overload, it becomes congested with a staccato of telegraphic signals trying desperately to keep up with the input of frightened messages from all sides. The more subtle harmonics of the heart become lost as the responsibility for control gets thrown increasingly onto the mind. But if this frantic activity is stilled for long enough, the tone of the heart becomes audible again and recovers its original power of resonance. It will return only if the voice that finally finds its way through the layers of protection has no hidden agenda, no intention to manipulate, and no goal except to convey the truth as directly as it can.

Although I do not pretend to understand all that goes on in this mysterious world of resonance, I believe that each individual holds within the self, whether hidden or overt, a unique vibration, a unique combination of harmonic tones. We all have the capacity, once the static is cleared, to tune in to what is tonally true, that is, to recognize without effort those voices that are organic and nurturing as well as those that have intent to do harm. Taking this for granted, there seem to be two levels of awareness in the healing process that operate at the same time. The first centers around the tone of support required to address the sensory centers of the body directly. It is a tone that must bypass the mind, because the mind will always try to interfere by making intellectual order out of anything that is going on. The quality of this tone varies from person to person and depends upon the initial response to silence as well as upon the degree of fear and distrust involved. The tone may require many words or no words at all; it may require a gentle approach or one full of strength and authority; it may require a deliberately slow pace or repartee that is lightning fast. It is a tone that matches the identity of the being in its uninhibited mode, a tone that challenges or entreats the original, confident voice to come out of hiding. The other level has to do with challenging the overlay of voices that have been developed as forms of protection. It is a matter of playing theater with them, exaggerating them, replacing them, even mocking them if necessary, in order to expose them for what they are, thus drawing the person towards recognizing their alien quality. Within the interplay of these two levels, there develops simultaneously an exorcism of substitute voices and a rediscovery of the original tones before they were taken over. In the initial stages the true tone acts as a clearing of the way, as a pre-echo for the memory to return to. Then, as the process continues and the individual begins to respond to true tone again, the voice-play begins. For example, this play may center around an oft-repeated phrase that, through the mouth of some authority figure, has haunted the child for a long time. From phrases such as these come the key moments of cut off and change, moments when the child stifled its instinctive response and substituted some conciliatory tone. It is this instinctive response that is often the first sign of the organic voice returning, and it may burst out in startling and unfamiliar style. These are responses that have likely been lost for years, responses that sometimes need to be repeated over and over again in order to make up for the number of times they have been swallowed down. Once they can find their way back up the throat and out the mouth again, they clear the way for many more, allowing the original censored vocabulary to be gradually restored.

It is then that the musical quality of the voice begins to make itself known. We are all born with music in us, however personal its nature, and I only need to hear a healthy baby sounding to know that originally there never was much distinction between language and music, between speech and song. The baby takes in the quality of tone through the heart long before beginning to understand the meaning of words through the mind. At that time all sound has the same potential as music anyway, offering the same subtle variations of melody, harmonics and rhythm. But when words and meaning enter in before the music is given a chance to establish on its own, the lyrical quality will soon be replaced by a non-musical vein. The need to make logical sense will intrude on the musical tone and the heart will lose its resonating power. It becomes very clear, when music informs the voice, why certain people's speaking tones can never be ignored, why they demand attention simply because of the way they sound. A certain tone of voice, when it coincides with a certain moment of vulnerability in another person, can have a deep effect, regardless of the meaning of the words. For words are first of all carriers of sound, vehicles quite beyond the power that any meaning can give to them. It is this sound that enters some dark abandoned cavern deep within the soul and, through the power of its reverberations, reactivates all the life, light and mystery that has been hidden there. Which brings me back to my own child, the inveterate liar, struggling with truth and falsehood for so many years, waging the family war of right and wrong, quite unaware of the music left behind, of the time before meaning when lying had no framework on which to work its tortuous designs. •

VIII. TOUCH

Voice and touch: they go together. They are the source of a child's security. From the beginning of life they are the ground on which strength and sensitivity are founded. Without the nourishment from these two elements little else can begin to grow.

There was a man who came to see me for the first time several years ago. He was waiting outside my room and I was running late. So I stepped outside for a brief moment and called out, "I'll be with you in a few minutes." I then returned to the room to finish the current session. He let me know later that, at the first sound of my voice, while he was still waiting outside, he began to cry. He came into the room crying, and all I did for a full hour was to hold him and rock him as he sobbed and wailed in my arms. For the following three sessions more or less the same thing happened and only then could he express himself in words, could talk about his pain and his despair. I do not fully understand the timing of that kind of release, but there was no question in my mind that, through the simplest stimulus of voice and touch, he was called back to the very beginning of his life to recreate for himself the support foundations that he had never been given. So starved had he become for those basic necessities that the body, at a moment's invitation, leapt back forty years to recover the essentials that had been lost. It was not that he was unable, from this ungrounded state, to put a mask on for the world, but he had lost all sense of direction and purpose inside. He was drifting into a kind of limbo state because he could not find a line back to those basic physical requirements he had been deprived of as a child.

Things have become murky and confused around touch. It is probably the area in which human beings are least clear and most afraid. There are obvious reasons for this, not the least of which is the uncertain division between sexual and non-sexual touch and therefore the fear that any kind of physical contact is going to lead to impossible complications. This is a very real state of affairs and the fears are not unfounded, but it is a great pity nonetheless. The worst consequence of such fears is that touch becomes separated off or eliminated as part of the healing process; meaning that the most natural, the most essential form of life support is taken away. It is true that the quality of touch required for a baby to feel secure has, for the most part, not been available; so already a powerful instinct is at work in the untouched person to find some kind of replacement wherever it can be found. Often what the person is looking for is actually very simple. It is to feel the physical presence of someone else and rest in the security of that contact. It is to feel again some form of physical grounding so that the body can relax in reassurance of its own sensory existence.

This kind of primal need is about as far from sexual desire as can be found. Although the confusion is more understandable if it is seen how readily sex becomes a substitute for the original craving. Thus, in search of a simple form of physical contact, a person may first project an energy that is strongly sexual. This exaggerated sexual energy is often a sign that the individual has given up believing that the need for touch can be satisfied in any other way. The sexual channel, the seductive mode, has at least been tried and proven to give a certain amount of contact, has satisfied a bare minimum of needs; but anything more complete, any deeper sense of rest has been relinquished altogether. For this reason much of the sexual energy has become a mask, a protective veneer that hides the deeper need of the child to be held in safety, to be taken in physically without further, more complicated expectations. So it is important to clear the way for this simplicity to show itself again and for the uncomplicated physical holding to be accessible as it ought to have been long ago. To eliminate touch in an atmosphere that, by its very nature, encourages other forms of intimacy is as unnatural as what is most feared: some kind of unclear sexual engagement between the two people involved. If this indeed happens, it is clear that both have become enmeshed in the workings of the mask and, for that reason alone, the child's re-emergence is doomed. But if there is a move to the other extreme and touch is altogether eliminated, the most natural of all forms of communication is eliminated also.

If it is possible to come to terms with these initial fears and be completely clear that any kind of sexual interference is a travesty of the process at hand, touch has as much subtlety and range to offer as sound. It involves a direct transmission of energy that accompanies and blends with whatever other form of contact is going on. However, it goes without saying that each individual's prior experience with touch has to be taken into consideration. Just as prolonged silence can provoke a range of reaction, so touch can also, and there are times when it is the last element required in a situation; when all it does, despite intentions of gentleness, is to reactivate in the person a memory of past physical cruelty. Whatever the quality of touch in the present, it will immediately take on the color of the past, so deeply has the previous experience been branded into the system. So physical trust can take a long time to establish and may, in certain cases, never be established at all. Physical sensitivity requires the utmost respect and the initiation of contact left entirely in the other's hands. With voice it is conceivable to enter right away, even if the audible channels have been interfered with, but with touch the sensory circuit seems to take longer to recover. Often the very safety of non-touch, the presence of someone who activates no danger of unwanted intrusion, is sufficient for physical relaxation to begin.

Here I am referring to those people who instinctively withdraw from any kind of touch whatsoever. They keep themselves away from physical contact as much as they can because of the memory of insensitive handling at an early age and because of a hypersensitivity of their own that has never received adequate respect or care. But there are others who respond to the same kind of careless handling in a very different way. They develop layers of protection in sensitive areas of their body and so when touched, register very little response at all. There is no fear of contact in the moment because a desensitization has already taken place, numbing the body out and reducing to a considerable degree its powers of physical reception. Touch will not be of much use to these people despite its caring quality because the being's inner core is deeply hidden behind these dense layers of protection. All that can be done in this case is to watch for the body's opening, become aware of the chinks in the armor and encourage the sensitivity as it begins to come alive again. Touch is often very welcome as this aliveness returns, for there is great relief when the body begins to feel again. Whether it be the heart, the throat or the belly, there are certain points of contact that can be made in order to draw emphasis to previously neglected areas. Touch becomes a conduit through which energy can be returned to the system, often drawing with it a rush of emotional energy also. Whatever moment of life is being regathered, there is likely to be a corresponding physical center; in the throat, perhaps, if it has to do with the difficulty of sound rising up, or in the heart if it is a matter of reconnecting to the pain of love. And between these various centers there are connecting lines to be traced that can ease the area from its feelingless isolation and allow the original sensations to return. It is a way of keeping track of the re-emergence of the body and ascertaining that it synchronizes with the quicker movement of the spirit and the emotions. The spirit travels considerably faster than the body and there are times when the one can extensively outrun the other, leaving the body crying out for some acknowledgement of its own slower speed, crying out in pain at the strain of separation and the impatience of its owner who will not pay attention to the warning signals. Touch brings notice to the body's needs, speaks the body's language in such a way that it will listen and re-integrate with the spirit before the separation becomes too extreme.

But of course all bodies are different and require a different quality of touch. There is a physical aura that is unique to each person and to align with that aura means to discover those particular parts of the body that act as primary conductors of energy. It is a matter of identifying their language and listening to the different stories they have to tell. In some it is the hands, in some the jaw, in others an unusual elegance in the turn of the neck. Sometimes it is only in movement that the body makes itself known, but it is often the more subtle signals, whether moving or still, that lead to the depth of physical dialogue that is required. They might lead to a sudden urge to roll over and wrestle on the floor; or to hold both feet firmly as encouragement to ground; or simply a light touch on the shoulder or the hand. It might feel right to act on the impulse right away or delay it for a time until a more obvious opening is available. Whatever form the physical language takes or does not take, it cannot be ignored; it is a form of interaction that is a continuously open line, ready to give information at a moment's notice.

It is also a quick way of getting to know the complexities of a person's nature. For example, in almost everyone there is a quality of physical magnetism that the body uses to lure people in its direction. It instinctively encourages contact by bringing forward what it believes to be its most attractive part. This can make itself known through a gesture, through a distinctive mannerism, or simply through a certain look in the eye. It comes across without inhibition or need for encouragement and makes itself available as an immediate and confident point of connection. However, the part that readily comes forward is likely to be compensating for another part that remains hidden, a part that has been lurking in the background for many years without daring to reveal its fears. To observe one is to be on the way to observing the other, because it is likely that together they have formed a conspiracy of protection; and much can be discovered if the conspiracy is broken open and the hidden aspect encouraged to come out of hiding. For example, a man may be accustomed to meeting the world with his jaw, demanding, it would seem, an aggressive form of contact, while a glance at his hands, perhaps hidden behind his back, will give evidence of a much softer inclination. The true nature may not thrive on challenge so much as on gentle touch. To find gradual contact through the hands may then open a passage to soften the jaw and expose a less aggressive demeanor. In the same way a woman may lead first with her mouth in an expression of disappointment or resignation, when it is actually the shoulders that bear the power; and when the shoulders find their true expression, a strength and stature will emerge that might give to the mouth a very different character. As the process continues, a physical balance re-asserts itself, drawn out by touching of those parts that have remained shy. They need to be given courage by the sensitive touch of another human being before they can risk revealing their natural state.

But perhaps the most vital function of physical contact is at moments of emotional stress, moments when the body risks dipping into memories of great pain and exposing its potential disintegration in the presence of someone else. These are steps down into the body's chaos, descent into altogether unpredictable manifestations that are evidence of the physical suffering that has been endured. In this situation the subtlety of presence, voice and touch is paramount, but that of touch is perhaps the most delicate of all. In this state every nerve-ending is raw to an excruciating degree and any shift in the sensory field is felt in like proportion. Often full presence is sufficient in itself because that is the basis of the child's need, but there are times when a delicate contact through the body can make all the difference, when even the simple pressure of a hand in a particular way allows the system to take in the reality of the support, creating confirmation that one is not this time alone. Yet more than the slightest gesture can already be too much, because as soon as the freedom of space is violated, as soon as there is forced pressure from another's energy, there is danger of close-down and withdrawal. For example, there is usually enormous resistance to being cared for in a demeaning way, one that does not bring with it complete alliance with the suffering state. There is also an extreme sensitivity to the supporter's own emotional stability, a concern that he or she may need taking care of at any point in the process. So there can be no reservations or half-measures in this alliance. Any uncertainty of touch is likely to instill anxiety rather than confidence. Furthermore, the uncertainty is likely to bring back the negative aspects of touch that set off the insecurity in the first place. But when the support is clear and unhesitating, a free-flowing circuit develops between two people that opens up access to each other's emotional rhythms. It is a precise alignment that allows the gestures of support to form a momentary unification outside the normal limits of space and time. What begins as a delicate physical bridging ends in a powerful process of merging; contact of the slenderest nature leads to the deepest emotional core. This circulation of physical and emotional energy offers replacement for an endless cycle of solitude and a belief that full contact with other human beings can never be.

I have already described how I first found access to the hidden parts of myself through massage. It was only after my body had recovered its deep sensitivity to touch that the buried feelings could find their way through to the surface again. Since then my need for physical contact has lessened, but its priority stays the same. When my feelings move into a dangerously fragile extreme, to have words or explanations around me without touch only increases the isolation that takes me over when my emotions are that strong. Words in that state literally make no sense at all. However well intended, they only confuse matters more, reminding me of the cold barrage of logic that must have resisted my emotional disintegration as a child. For me it is simply confirmation of how separate the two worlds are, the world of those who become lost in the chaos of their own feelings versus the world of those who, in the face of them, remain distant and aloof. As my memory of that separation closes in, it is only a gentle, firm touch that can draw me out again, a simple gesture of compassion that gives me permission to fall apart without needing to explain anything. Often I do not know the cause myself and anyway it does not matter to know. The touch I feel is the touch of my own physical reality without objections from those on the outside. So, when the situation is reversed and I hold another in my arms, I am willing to extend the contact for a long time. I will sustain the physical line even when there is little external evidence that anything of import is going on inside. I do so because I know that touch can make the difference between what is bearable and unbearable, between fear of unutterable loss and the slim chance of finding a way back to solid foundations again. And the reward is to feel in the mutual closeness a new life stirring inside, to feel the line of contact reach down far enough to bring essential warmth to inaccessible places; like a fire rekindled at the core, hardly identifiable at first, then gradually spreading its warmth through all of the body's centers.

IX. TIMING

The elements of support I have explored so far are all integral components of an open space. They are active ingredients, but they are also, on another level, inactive in that they can be felt as part of the space before any form of dialogue gets underway. They emanate from the stillness and the silence, announcing themselves in advance and encouraging engagement to begin. The welcome this openness offers is a rare thing in itself. There are no obstacles to scramble over and no need for defense reflexes to spring into automatic operation. At the same time the resources that have been hidden deep down sense a new kind of permission extended to them.

Yet entry into this space can be somewhat of a shock at first. It is as if the being, accustomed to a carnival life in which insubstantial and distorted images are reflected from mirrors on all sides, now finds no reflections at all; only a feeling of having room to breathe and being buoyed up lightly by invisible hands. It is part of the shock of this entry that unconscious associations begin to take over, brief sensory reminders, for example, of those moments in life when some kind of nurturing was available; perhaps even a flash of what it was like to be seen. As these associations begin to return, time and space take on a different dimension. Both people, without being aware of the change, shift into a subtly altered state of consciousness through which a yearning for the truth is activated, a yearning that is willing, for the first time, to wrestle with all the many layers of fear. This immediate desire for the truth and the distortions of past experience come up against one another and demand to be re-aligned. It is a natural desire that takes over as soon as the flexibility of the open space makes its impact; for at the core there has always remained a consistent desire for the truth and a strong need to become acquainted with the information it has to offer.

The fastest I ever saw this open space operate on someone was with a woman who visited me quite recently. She was a person who had tried everything under the sun to bring some kind of order and meaning to her life but, despite all efforts, was still overwhelmed by an unbearable fear. By the time she came to see me her system showed an exhaustion that could have only come about through years of terror. She took me in with one steady, intense gaze and with hardly a pause, plunged deep within herself to replay a horrendous scene from her childhood. She continued to play out one scene after the other, all of them prelude to a violent rape that she endured when she was six years old. Until this very moment, all these incidents had been completely blocked from her memory. Yet when permission and space were finally given her to re-enter them, every awful, living detail was accessible as if no time had passed since they had happened. They had been buried for years inside of her, playing themselves out in slow motion in the unconscious of her memory over and over again and causing this constant condition of unplaceable terror. Once she was able to place the memories within the real continuity of her life, she was released from the extremity of her fear. While she re-enacted her life in this astounding way, I did absolutely nothing, except to ensure she had adequate protection around her while she physically thrashed around. Her being had longed for many years to recover this truth about herself, and the desperation itself was ample provocation for the speed with which she acted. But, with all her longing, she had never found a clear enough environment through which to reclaim the intense cruelty of those early years. She had barely been able to survive without them, leaping over into a fantasy frame of existence that refused to entertain the possibility of such outrageous assault. The pressure she had brought to bear against herself for not living the way she believed she ought was an added impediment. It was this pressure, above all, that the open space had the power to dissolve. As soon as it was gone, as soon as it had literally fallen away, she did the whole thing entirely herself. Most of the time, on a conscious level, she must have been hardly aware that I was in the room with her, yet she knew exactly what to do. It was, in the simplest of terms, true energy circulating, the discovery of a circuit that finally had no interference on the line.

This is an example of support working in a relatively inactive mode and of the power it has, as setting only, to bring the hidden experience of life to the surface. But it is unusual for the desire for truth to kick in that fiercely and directly, unusual for it to require no extra encouragement at all. In most cases, the giving of courage plays a strong role, and it is at these moments that timing plays such an essential role. Timing is the rhythm through which presence, safety, voice and touch are set in motion; it is the active interplay of these elements. It is what gives a meeting between people the same characteristics as dance or music. Each meeting has its own kind of rhythm and its own quality of motion, depending on the nature of the people involved and the dynamics of the process at hand. Whatever the interchange, it is not what is spoken that lies at the center, but the subtlety of movement underlying the words, the rhythmic pattern that has to keep changing to keep pace with the constant shifting of the being inside. If, for example, touch is involved, it has to be synchronous with these rhythmic patterns of change, sensitive to whatever other elements of safety and support are in that moment required. These rhythmic patterns can sometimes be identified by the way a person comes into a room, but external manifestations may be deceptive; more telling is a less obvious energetic frequency that transmits to the space a particular atmosphere and tone. It is an inner rhythmic pulse that establishes itself right away, creating movement in the space when before there was none. This initial quality of motion sets the mood, is prelude to any subsequent fuller engagement. An essential aspect of support is to adapt to and become one with this inner rhythm as quickly as possible. In this way a person can, as never before, put a claim on the space without feeling any answering resistance.

Already the dance has begun, and from the moment of slipping into another's rhythm an instinctive sense of timing becomes possible. This timing involves a sensory form of listening that is as essential to theater as it is to life. As far as theater goes, it is only through this sense of timing that the actors find a clear passage through to the audience who can then immerse themselves in the intimacy of the exchange. It is the essence through which actors and audience mutually pace one another so that the meeting can be complete. When the timing is off, when the rhythms lose their synchronization, the closeness of intimacy is cut off. In the theater it is the actor's skill and experience that hold it all together, that sustains this rhythmic synchronization. Every nuance counts; a beat too long or too short makes all the difference because there is, in each individual moment of connection, a quality of resonance that goes home. This is not a do-or-die situation, for there is such a wide range of possibility involved; but there is an infinite subtlety about this timing, a subtlety that can be endlessly refined. The level of intimacy in any exchange, in life as well as theater, can rest on the careful nuance of a phrase, on the delicate inflection of a word, on the precise shaping of a gesture. It is also dependent on the initial quality of silence and stillness in which every form of expression is clothed. A word out of rhythm can interrupt a flow of communication already established, while the same word placed differently can move like lightning to the heart.

It is this potential for intimate contact that brings theater and life so close together. The intensity of contact that people look for in the movies or any kind of live performance is not very different from the intimacy we crave with each other. Both move us to a depth that is inaccessible any other way. Yet it has to be recognized that the intimacy of life involves a much greater risk. In theater the form is there to protect us; it allows us our intimate entry, our private communion, then it is all over and we can retreat again. This is not so in personal relationships, and for that very reason opening to one another's rhythms is a relatively dangerous venture. It creates opportunity for barriers to come down, but simultaneously exposes the risk of advantage being taken. We have been long conditioned to such expectations, conditioned also to resisting the rhythms of other people because, as a child, they took us over so completely. The rhythms of a young child are very fragile and easily overrun by the insensitive timing of others. They seldom have a chance to establish themselves with any confidence because they are forced so early into an adaptive mode, losing track of the intimate connection they were hoping to establish in the first place. So for people to come into an environment in which they can immediately claim the space as their own is often a fearful experience before it is a freeing one, and the sense of danger will remain until there is clear evidence that support is intended rather than invasion. This will be communicated only if the rhythm of exchange has not already been chosen and if it is at the other's pace that all moves are made towards a more intimate connection.

Once these rhythms are established, what has to be considered is whether they constitute a natural mode of existence or whether they have been taken on by force of circumstance; either, for example, through a strongly influential figure in the person's past or through a work situation that has demanded an extreme degree of adaptation. This last is a surprisingly common phenomenon, particularly in a situation where men have automatically moved into a slot their fathers, or even their grandfathers, occupied before them. In these cases the rhythms of their lives have been pre-ordained for them, regardless of the individual nature at hand. There was one man who came in once whose rhythm was unusually fast. There was a constantly rushing quality about him. He would often be late, arriving on the run, panting with exhaustion, and while he was with me would consult the clock at regular five minute intervals. Time literally possessed him, someone else's time. He desperately tried to keep pace with it, but always seemed to be running behind. He had never for one moment in his life paused to consider his own rhythms and it was only gradually that they began to appear to him. However, they could not begin to do so until I had given space to the rushing man, given him the opportunity to literally play himself out. Once his rhythm was given an opportunity to express itself without counter-pressure of any kind, it discovered for itself its degree of belonging or not belonging. Provided the space remained open, the true rhythm made itself known and entered into battle with the assumed rhythm in order to claim its rightful place. This man had long been running on his father's rhythms and his father's work patterns as he remembered them. He had taken on both and, because his nature was so different, the results were utterly exhausting him. Over a period of time it became clear to him that his natural rhythms were about as slow as anyone's could be. He had been brought up in the hubbub of a large city when he was actually quiet and simple at heart, someone who's true nurturing existed in the sensuality and slow rhythms of nature herself. A year later he had no interest in the clock and found, to his gratification, a quiet, almost monk-like existence through which he could carry on, in a completely different rhythm and setting, his original career.

In this kind of gradual transformation, when the rhythms that are functioning are so far away from the original nature, the role of timing becomes complex indeed. For at the heart of the process lies a brutal opposition, the waging of an out-and-out war. A certain point will arrive when the imposed rhythms will hang on for dear life, particularly when they sense that the natural ones are serious in their efforts to re-emerge. It is at this stage that strong encouragement is necessary in the form of an alliance with the new-found tempo. There is a timing that belongs to the old part and a timing that belongs to the new, and the transition has to somehow be made between the two. This has little to do with the details of an individual's life, but concerns the inner dynamics that give motion to the being; the way body, gesture and voice tone interact in all forms of expression. The imposed rhythm is actually doomed to failure from the very beginning because there is no depth of resonance in its mode of presentation. It has the same kind of appeal as a caricature in the theater, a representative of some quality rather than a full-blooded character, and since it has no real roots, it can only operate within a limited range. But its very fixity gives it its own kind of strength, a strength that has allowed it to dominate for so long. The natural rhythms, on the other hand, are, as they re-emerge, more subtle and tentative in their expression and therefore need support to make themselves fully known. The kind of support they need is a shift of pace through suggestion, allowing pauses to hold for a longer period of time, for example, thus creating space for the new rhythms that have not yet found their flow. It is a process of jogging the memory, reminding it of rhythmic roots that do truly belong. All this needs a prelude of close listening, because only through the listening can details of the other's true rhythms be ascertained. They come in flashes at first, through sudden unfamiliar gestures or a word used in a different way, details which need to be marked for future reference, then fed back to the individual when the struggle with the imposed rhythms gets out of hand. The range of expression that can be discovered in this way can also bring with it flares of excitement, further indication of how much the range of life has been contained throughout the years. More fluidity of expression then streams into the system and a liveliness bubbles up that insists on its own free will.

There is one further aspect of timing. It has to do with a need to be constantly changing rhythms to suit the different phases of an individual's development. Throughout the whole process there is rarely much resting ground because the pace keeps changing all the time. This reflects the system's desire to keep exploring, like an actor building up a repertoire, extending the performing range. However, the speed of these changes is often difficult to keep up with. There are times when I believe I have found the support required: a certain quality of touch, perhaps, alternating with a carefully modulated vocal tone. Then all at once, for no apparent reason, a shift will occur and neither will serve any purpose whatsoever. They are rendered void, and there is nothing I know of in the moment that will take their place. I can only return to the open space and listen for where the next lead comes from, if it comes at all.

For example, there was one woman who initially needed a lot of touch, a lot of comfort through the touch which allowed for deep, wordless emotions to find release. Then without warning the touch was rejected and replaced by an insistent demand for information. A rhythm of almost harsh interrogation came out of this need, a fiery succession of questions and answers. This was followed by a period of absolute silence, whole hours in which there was no visible movement or exchange at all; just two people hanging out together with no expectations that anything need openly happen between them. Out of this suddenly, one day, came an outpouring of words. They went on and on and whenever I made an attempt to speak myself, the rhythms that she was trying to establish for herself were altogether ruined. She told me so in no uncertain terms and more or less put a gag on me. At first I could not believe that anything constructive was happening in this phase. I could not accept that this particular rhythm required so little participation on my side. I could not trust, until considerably later, that a vital energy was circulating within that form of non-exchange. After being interrupted and crowded in on all her life, the woman was finally taking the opportunity to say her all with a stream of words that seemed like they would never end. But they ended as abruptly as every other phase, and at the moment of their completion a new kind of presence emerged. It was so impressive that it appeared to fill double the usual space and I realized with a certain shock that I was sitting with a whole person for the first time. It seemed that all the various rhythms she had been exercising had made a decision to gather together in the one being and were now showing me their combined strength. And, whether or not I was willing to acknowledge it at the time, every phase had participated in the final whole. I existed as the sounding board for each variation, one that required only an adjustment of rhythm and tone as each phase came to meet me.

It is the recovery of these rhythms and their integration within a single complex being that lie at the heart of true intimacy. By true intimacy I do not mean intimacy with others, although that follows naturally, but with oneself. It is an intimacy that leads to an ease and celebration of all the expressive parts of oneself. People reveal themselves only in proportion to the amount of freedom and attention they feel around them. The fuller the permission, the greater the possibility for expansion, and the dance of life will not find its appropriate rhythms until someone else's attention and understanding are fully there. Without them trust in one's own natural timing will never be established and what often takes its place is an impossible awkwardness, a fear that any form of public exposure will make one appear like a fool. This personal intimacy, this rhythmic integrity, affects every moment of our daily lives. It is the quality that creates out of time a naturally flowing river, a continuity from one moment to another, from one experience to another, even though each experience is very different. Despite the ever-changing rhythms, transitions can always be found, a continuum of fluctuating energy that carries us along. The result is life as an inner dance of passion to a personal drumbeat that is always changing time; also permission for the fullest extension of that dance, no matter how different the dances of others may be.

Part Three. Exploring

X. JOURNEY INTO THE DARK

To explore from these foundations in a way that does not impose too many limitations, and in a way that also does justice to the many levels of sensitivity, is first of all a challenge of words. For there is no language I yet know of that can express the intricacies of human change. In the first part I have told something of my own experience that has helped me towards these discoveries. In the second I have talked about the supportive environment that allows people to open to themselves and show more of who they are so that the vital process of expansion can begin. In both these parts I have written so as to convey an orderly connection between things. My intention has been to provide a continuum through which events from my past and their influence are described and certain observations laid out clearly. But once the journey begins inside, once the process of expansion gets underway, there are no straight lines to be followed and few definable conclusions to be drawn.

What I am dealing with from now on is a growing complexity, a phenomenon that is closest to a particular kind of poetry or fiction, to *The Scarlet Letter*, for example, where images interweave in an ever-increasing ambivalence of design. To write of human nature clinically, to set up rules and categories, has never made much sense to me because it is so constantly subject to movement and change. As soon as it enters into its own largeness, it literally takes off, committing itself to a certain course of expansion and in the process defying any attempts that are made to hold it still. Provided the process of expansion is allowed to continue, there will always be new territory to be explored and always a deepening of life's design. There is no such thing as completion.

The advantage of a poetic approach is a language that moves as the subject moves, and if I were a Hawthorne, I would bring a new form into existence so that the interweave of human existence could be given the play and depth of exploration that it deserves. To simplify at this stage would not be useful. It would foster the illusion that we can hold the truth captive, rather than admitting the fact that truths are perpetually evolving principles that keep changing in the same way we change. So, given that language has little power to capture the subtleties of this inner design, it may at least be able to move in and around them and catch glimpses of the act of creation as creation turns.

What makes us rich as human beings is our experience. What has impoverished us is having too much of that experience discredited and taken away. Most of it has been buried in shame and guilt and is fiercely held under by judgments that we have taken on from others and still systematically apply to our own daily lives. The richness is already there; it is our attitude that has imprisoned us. A long, long history of authoritarian figures has decreed that a small percentage of those riches may be all right, but the majority is highly suspect, although a portion of it is perhaps salvageable if we say how sorry we are and admit how bad we have been. The result of this history is severely squeezed human beings, unable to understand how they came to be that way or why life seems to keep offering such limited horizons. The unexpected part is that, along with these cramped sensations, there are echoes of memory that occasionally return to us, hinting at the possibility of a very different design. It is because those echoes have survived that people come for assistance, wanting to know if they are tantalizing illusions, one further deception in a whole series of deceptions, or whether they have something substantial to offer after all.

It is at great risk that these people come, and their arrival bears witness to the fact that, despite so much misguided authority, a line is still connected to the depth of themselves. They could just as well let this connection go, give up on it altogether; but instead they have chosen to follow it into the dark to find out if there is any verifiable substance at the other end. It is a moment of critical decision, a moment when all previous influences will be seriously challenged and submitted to long-term examination. Enormous amounts of energy are required to do this. It is a leap of faith, a leap that carries people away from all the mighty external structures they have become dependent on and has them latch onto a single thread that barely connects them to their own personal source.

This decision is all the more remarkable in that a great deal of pain and loss is involved. Not that the process of operating on such a small percentage of the self is without pain. In fact, it often has to become more or less unbearable for this measure of decision to come their way. But that pain is a different kind of pain; it is a pain of losing touch altogether, a giving up. The pain they invite by trusting in that single remaining thread of themselves is the pain of coming back to life, the raw rush of rejected sensitivity returning. It is a journey to the underside without guarantee that there is a way back out into the clear. It is also a journey into a world where there are no definitive answers and never will be, a world that offers neither models for future behavior nor a collective ordering of what is right and what is wrong. This involves throwing over much of what has been advertised as riches and trusting that this slender connection will provide a substitute considerably more worthwhile. All the odds are against this happening because there are, as yet, no guaranteeable signs of stability; only an increase of fear and pain and a cloudy, unattractive fragment of a life hovering just out of range.

This is one approach: a line into the unknown self, offering only the slenderest evidence of nourishment. A perspective from the outside looking in.

(II)

But there is another perspective, from the inside looking out. Change the angle of approach and a different landscape appears.

From this perspective it is like looking out on unexplored territory from behind the bars of a prison. This prison takes the form of suffocation through structures that have never belonged to the independent self, and only now announce themselves as too alien to be endured. Until recently this unexplored territory has appeared relatively uninteresting and very far away. There has been no reason even to examine it very closely, let alone consider a move in its direction. But as the forms become more and more confining and irrelevant, the landscape beyond takes on a more inviting quality, even offering opportunity for some kind of release. There is still a lot of fear, but it is not the same kind of fear as before. It has an edge of excitement and with it there is a stirring of curiosity, a long-lost friend. From behind the heavy bulwarks of families, traditions and religions details appear on the other side for the first time and the imagination wonders if it can slip unnoticed through the space between the bulwarks and venture a few steps beyond. Along with this fantasy comes the remote possibility of existence without the terror that these bulwarks have always insisted on as a means of maintaining their power. It is a powerful flight of fancy and the strongest encouragement yet for those first tentative steps from behind the bars. So in trepidation the first steps are taken until, in sudden recoil, comes a nasty jolt of recognition: large though the fear of the oppressor has been, the fear of the unknown looms larger still. For to risk those boundaryless spaces means giving up all familiar reference to the outside, means trusting that the impulse from the inside will bring along sufficient information to act as its own dependable guide.

And so begin the swirling doubts, the hesitations, the helplessness and a new kind of pain. But already there is no return. Despite the pain and the confusion, the territory beyond remains strangely compelling and there is so much further to go. Besides, there is a new kind of beauty that signals from afar.

Given this delicate testing of new ground, it is obvious why some kind of assistance is required. But what is to be its nature and who are the authority figures now? Certainly not the familiar dispensers of law and order, not the sources of power around which people have been used to gathering in order to have their questions answered and their problems solved. No more is there that separation between those who know and those who don't know, between the so-called enlightened masters and those who follow behind. There can be no more separation because it has led inevitably to a giving over of the self to others and so to a loss of power, a diminishment of the individual authority that was given at birth. And because that separation has existed, there has been no chance to discover the double dimension of our own natures, that essential interplay between the part that is human and the part that is divine. For the human being is simultaneously unknower and all-knower, the bumbler knocking heads with the sublime; and it is the realization of this lively relationship inside that gives the necessary courage to continue exploration of new ground. To leave the familiar need for authority behind is to find one's own way, and in the process an old concept of hierarchical teaching is turned upside down. Teaching and learning join as one in individual acts of curiosity and desire, substituting for that obsession to impose knowledge and insist on its relevance to all situations and all of mankind.

The fear continues, but it is manageable now, provided no pressure is brought to bear. Previously this fear has been difficult to handle because it has been created by dire warnings from the wielders of power to whom knowledge has been given away. What could have been open territory available for exploration at any time was marked as forbidden land, the place where judgments descend before the ground can even be tested to see if its foundations are firm. These warnings are now an internal voice constantly objecting that every place is the wrong place to be. And this voice will only fade away if someone else stands alongside, listening to the voice, aware of the voice, but interposing nothing. Within the nothing, within the waiting, within the new curiosity stirring ever so slightly beneath the waiting, the old structures begin to fall away.

Curiosity can tolerate fear of the unknown provided it has some stable presence through which to circulate its concerns. But it cannot live with the fear of others' authority and power, with the belief that the knowledge of others comes first and what the self discovers under its own initiative has little bearing on the matter. It was not long before Christ's encouragement towards self-knowledge, his priority of "know thyself", became swamped by his followers' insistence on hell and damnation as a means of controlling individual desire. What began as a path to freedom, a sense of new possibilities, ended up as a narrow bed of fear, a tool of power to prevent people from nurturing their own individuality and owning the potential they found there. The same process of contraction happens in families when the child reaches out at a young age towards new things and is immediately cut off by those in charge. They have to confine its explorations to what they themselves are familiar with, and in this way perpetuate the division between knowing and unknowing, between the authority of any given structure and those who both want and fear to move beyond its limits. This gap leaves no opportunity for true interchange. It prevents the possibility of an ideal situation developing: everyone communicating from a state of unknowing, everyone released from fear of right and wrong, from fear as the fiercest stranglehold of life itself.

When released from these old concepts, keeping people company on life's journey is a matter of great finesse. It is not about telling anyone what to do; it is not even about presenting ideas through which they might improve their lives. It is closer to standing ignorant beside them and acknowledging with them their full sweep of responses to the unknown. It is closer still to lending courage to a gradual process of reduction, helping identify the layers that do not belong so that they can begin to fall away. For it is only what does not belong that is initially identifiable, and even then the identification seems to take on its own momentum, executing its own clearing as life's buried secrets rise to the surface of their own accord and lie exposed for the first time. In this process there is no knowledge as such, but rather a mutual agreement on what does not provide energy anymore or have any useful function to fulfill. It is a matter of reduction rather than accumulation, clearing the way backwards through time for the true self to catch sight of itself again and re-engage with life on its own terms.

(III)

There are two people I know for whom this return seemed an impossible feat. It seemed impossible because, no matter how far we travelled back together, no matter how much of themselves they recognized did not belong, the original curious self refused to come clear. It peeked out for moments, but not long enough to establish the confidence required for life to become a truly adventurous proposition. The fears of naked exposure remained too strong.

When I was with one of them a few months ago, I felt this lost state more immediately than I ever had before and with an instinctive gesture put my hand on her heart. In so doing I had the sensation, as I never had before, that there was no skin and bone between my hand and her heart, as if I had made contact directly with a tenuously delicate organ that barely had the courage to beat out loud. Along with this I felt it craving for warmth, rising to meet my hand in a desperate plea to be cradled, wanting the use of my extended arm as a life-line of support through which to beat more boldly. This was not the first time that I had touched her heart, but it was the first time it had given voice to itself in this way, had dared to let the tenuous degree of its survival be known. She was able, during that brief period of contact, to put words to the experience more clearly than I could. She spoke of how she longed for that line of warmth to be there for her always, longed for it to give her undeniable evidence that she could sustain a long-term connection with other living beings. Her loneliness was so intense at times that she had completely lost faith in her power to connect to other people. Knowing her history as I did, I could feel the harsh reality of what she was saying.

Here was someone who had had structure ruthlessly imposed on her from the first day of her life. She was one of those babies I mentioned earlier who cried continuously for the first two months of her life. As first child, her mother did not know what to do with her and to allay her fears, created a rigid schedule that she had taken out of a book. The order and routine, strictly adhered to, were the mother's salvation and the baby's hell. The mother's salvation because the baby eventually quieted down and became the perfect child; the baby's hell because all her natural rhythms were torn away from her before she had any opportunity to find out what they were. She went on to become the model eldest child in a strict Catholic family of five, taking vows as a nun when she was sixteen and sustaining the same rigid structure for herself over the next twelve years. This protection remained foolproof until her religious faith began to fall apart. Along with her faith all other forms disintegrated also and, in a state of panic, she was left to go all the way back to the beginning in search of a time when the structures of others had not regulated her life. It was a hard journey indeed, for there was no moment of relief except during the first months of violent protest at being forced onto her mother's routine. All her energy, however, had been consumed by protest and none had remained for discovery.

This was not exactly an encouraging situation, yet what surprised me in that moment of contact with her was the unmistakable signal that her heart, after all those years of neglect, still wanted to feel, still had a yearning for some source of warmth that would give it connection again. Where, I wondered, did this formless desire come from, and how could it still imagine some semblance of security within such a tenuous hold? I have no answer, but I do know that, with such slight foundation, any reconnection to an independent life source is an excruciatingly slow process that may never find completion. For all the cruelty that many children suffer, there is nothing as elusive or as hard to identify as absence. To be able to recollect and pinpoint harsh treatment, to come to terms with life as a war zone, is hard enough; but to grope in a vacuum around what appears to be a perfectly ordered family is perhaps most difficult of all. There is no substance to grab onto, no clear reason for the panic and misery that often catches up with those concerned only long after the original disconnection. Quite suddenly a responsible adult life seems impossible to take on, and there is no immediate evidence as to why it should be riddled with so much pain and helplessness. If there are obvious marks of conflict in a child's experience, at least it means there has been, at some time, some assertion of will and independence. But if imposed structures overwhelm before any form of articulation has begun, then the quirk of curiosity seems lost forever and with it the belief in existence as an autonomous being. To make matters worse, the child, when it has given up its own autonomy, gets into the habit of yearning for more structure from the outside as time goes on. More and more it becomes a case of voluntary confinement; a passive acceptance of a limited world with, more often than not, aggressive tendencies leaking out the side.

The second person is an orphan. He was taken away from his mother for adoption when he was a few days old and only recently, at the age of thirty, has found the courage to research his beginnings and find out the true facts of his birth. By initiating this journey to his own source he has begun an alarming venture into the void. During the last time I spent with him he evoked in very powerful terms the vastness and impersonality of the galaxy, the dark emptiness of space that surrounded him. The planet Earth was for him a mere speck in that emptiness and he himself an even smaller speck, altogether lost and indistinguishable from the other specks around him. And there was nobody who had control over this random, friendless existence and nobody who could relieve him from his suffering. This was no intellectual theorizing or idle speculation, but a severe emotional upheaval inducing in the body a fearful and uncontrollable trembling.

It was not surprising to find out that this man, up to this point in his life, had been in frantic search for one guru after another, any self-professed figurehead who would give him all the answers and save him from his doom. What was progressively disturbing to him was the failure of these gurus to support him. He has a brilliant mind and with uncanny cleverness picked up on the slightest shortcoming of any system of belief that was put before him. So, before long all these initially impressive figureheads had revealed unacceptable fallibilities. The more they fell by the wayside, the more angry and disappointed he became. All of them, starting with his foster parents who had little idea of who he was, were substitutes for his urgent need for some true line of connection, people who could replace the original sudden rupture from his own source. He had to lay all these structures and expectations on himself in order to fill the unbearable void that the original bereavement created. Eventually he had to disconnect from the expectation that any help was available. He had to take himself backward into the uncaring cosmos and face reality in a new way; take a good look at a world that provided no answers and would never come close to giving satisfaction to the wide range of his highly inventive mind.

It is somewhat ironic that these two people are linked in my mind by their brilliance, their originality and the sheer determination of their wills. It is a teasing paradox to recognize that the very people who have such a hard time connecting with their source are the ones who are extra quick and resourceful and thus unable, in the final event, to accept truth from anyone but themselves. Their awareness is too large and complex to be satisfied with anything other than what their own originality would offer them. So whatever external structure is sought after or imposed upon them is doomed to failure. Any single version of how life works is too small, too limited to encompass the depth of their own perceptions; and yet they are constantly overwhelmed by feelings of being unable to continue as self-sufficient members of the human race. They are signalling unceasingly, if erratically, out of the darkness, hazarding ingenious concepts of release that would satisfy anyone but themselves. And even though they continue to fail themselves, they never forsake a certain integrity of self-fulfillment that keeps them going through the depths of despair. All their attempts to cover themselves up have not worked, yet they will not be diverted through compromise from their original search for the truth.

For them it is a matter of do or die. Given the despair that both have encountered and continue to encounter, protection of some kind would seem essential. It would seem likely that they would choose at least one of the forms along the way as a more bearable means of living than the struggle of the desolate, unformed self. Even the fact that the forms kept falling away of themselves, leaving them no option but to engage in the nothingness of their origins, speaks eloquently to the determination of their journey. Maybe at the darkest point it becomes more of a death-wish than a journey. For self-search, at its deepest level, is almost bound to engage in a form of courtship with death. This courtship involves an ever-present opening to annihilation that must not be closed by false hopes or instructions from others about how to get through. Finally it is the reality of their own experience that they have to keep reaching for, and in extreme cases like these it is only through their own version of dying and being born again that wholeness can be regained. It is part of the integrity they have set up to see them through to the very end. Or the very beginning.

(IV)

But the presence of another can make a difference. Not between birth and death. There is no power there. But there **is** power in allowing such essential forces in people's lives to come together; in allowing them to move, change shape, and be visible in relationship together for the first time; in allowing them to exist outside the clutches of those who want to fix and separate them, thus paralyzing the search of the human soul and preventing it from going back as far as it needs to go.

Neither darkness nor death have a very good press. There has been a conspiracy going on for a long time to separate the light and the dark, as if the two have not always been inextricably woven together and dependent upon each other's existence. To separate them, to put them at war with each other, is to immediately set in motion the idea that the one has to be victorious over the other, that the one has to establish its dominion without the other, and above all, that one is acceptable while the other is not. Birth and death have suffered the same stigma of being unalterably divided, frozen into opposition so that there will always be the good experience and the bad experience conveniently polarized and ready at hand.

When someone is afraid of the dark and is joined by someone who is not, remarkable shifts can happen. All at once a completely unknown element is introduced that lets the being unwind from fear and the body slough off the influences associated with that fear. I do not know what happens when fear evaporates internally, when nothing is imposed on the being while it gropes in the dark for its own form, but the momentum is large. When I am close by, it feels like a clearing out of musty spaces and a fresh wind blowing through the channels between. Within these newly cleared spaces a major rearrangement of information begins, a reshuffling of what previously seemed impossible for the system to take in or understand. The associations, the distortions around light and dark, around birth and death, are very deep and can only rearrange themselves in a very deep chamber of the being. Some people will cling to any image connected with the light to avoid going deep into the underside of their own lives. At all cost they will avoid going to the place where such radical rearrangement is made welcome and opposites can regain such strong contact with one another that it becomes hard to distinguish between them. It is within this place of merging that support is found, far enough in to start all over again and allow for a renewed process of self-creation.

I was talking to a friend on the phone not long ago and during the conversation a bat flew into her house. She went into a panic and was desperate for it to leave. I asked her what she was afraid of and she said she was terrified it would "go for her" and tangle in her hair. It was what she had been warned would happen when she was very small. I began to tell her about my own fascination with bats and how, at an old house of mine in the mountains, I would spend time every evening at dusk watching the swooping grace of their flight. She was astonished. It had never occurred to her to watch them or be curious about them, and at that moment, while still on the phone, she began to do just that. The effect was instantaneous. "I can feel everything changing inside of me," she said with a certain wonder in her voice and lost all interest in removing the bat from her home.

XI. SENSITIVITY ASSAULTED

Wailing, like a mantra, repeated over and over again: "It wasn't meant to be like this. I don't understand. Why? Why? This is nothing like it was supposed to be. How did it come to be this way?"

"Was it different before?"

Stopping in surprise, "Before? I don't know. Before what?"

"Before it all became so impossible. Was there some other way you remember that was all right?"

Long pause. Puzzled expression, then face unexpectedly breaking into a smile. In the voice of a child, "Way back, you mean?"

"Yes. Way back. As far as you can go."

A surge of enthusiasm. "Everything was so ***interesting****."*

"Everything?"

Eyes suddenly alive as if seeing it all. "Oh yes. Everything. It was fascinating. So many colors. The day was so full."

"What do you mean, full?"

"Well, there was so much to do. There wasn't enough time to do it all in. So much I wanted to look at, to feel." Remembering again, the body joining with the memory. "Oh, the feelings!"

"What sort of feelings?"

Gasping, "Like bursting inside. There were so many I didn't know what to do with them all. A lot of rainbows. I wanted to tell everyone about the rainbows, show them all the colors. I wanted to find out if they saw them too."

"Did you tell them? Did you find out?"

Cutting off abruptly, the brightness of the face clouding over. "No. I tried. I wanted to so much. I couldn't." Long pause. "My father." Face changing, darkening, beginning to twitch with fear.

"What about him?"

No answer. Face convulsing. Tears.

"Did he yell at you?"

Shake of the head. More fear. A panic beginning to rise.

"Did he say anything at all?"

Another shake of the head. With difficulty, tremulous voice, "His face. It was his face. No, not only his face. His head too. It went all strange. Dark and scary inside, like this." An evocative gesture with both hands in front of the face. Twisting motion with the hands. Like trying to turn a corkscrew when the cork is too tight. The whole body shaking. Sudden scream. "No. Go away." Hands pushing out as if to ward off an attack, then a repeat of the corkscrew motion. Whispering, "Blackness inside his head. And his face like stone." Body in freeze-hold for a moment, face glowering, eyes turning hard and cruel. Then all at once collapse into grief. "I didn't do anything wrong. What did I do that was so wrong? I never meant to do anything wrong. It was all so beautiful, then–." Corkscrew with the hands again.

"Did the beauty come back when he went away?"

Shake of the head. Growling voice, angry. "He never went away."

"Never?"

Yelling, "Never!" Floods of tears, despair. "I was always terrified of doing something wrong. Terrified all the time that his face would be there again like that. I didn't know what I did wrong. I was laughing. I was so happy. There was so much beauty around. After that I was afraid all the time. And the beauty went away."

"No more colors?"

"No more colors." In a small voice, "I tried to be a good girl. I tried. I really did. I wanted him to smile. Then it would have been all right again. Then the darkness in his head would have gone away." Silence. Body scurrying into a corner, becoming very small, trying to disappear. "I tried so hard to make him smile. It never worked. I never saw him smile."

More silence. Small girl's face lost in despair. Then out of the despair a lament, not of the child or of the past, but a woman in the present furious at what her life has become. Voice full of both *rage and tears. "Do you know what happened when I parked my car this afternoon? I received my ticket from the parking attendant and put it under the visor. I* ***knew*** *I had put it under the visor. But when I stopped the car and turned the engine off, I sat there paralyzed with fear that I had lost it. In a panic I checked that it was there, but still the fear gripped me and I had to check again. Then I got out of the car and stood there, unable to close the door for fear that I would lock my keys inside. My keys were in my hand all the time, but that made no difference. I could not close the door. I stood there for the longest time rooted to the spot, unable to leave my car, still terrified that something had gone dreadfully wrong. How is it possible for me ever to believe that I have done something right? How do I know that I won't be making a fool of myself wherever I go? I cannot bear living my life in so much fear. I just cannot endure it any longer."*

(II)

When he entered the room, the first thing I noticed was the line of his jaw. He led with his jaw in a manner that immediately challenged everyone and everything he came in contact with. His eyes were distant, almost hostile, and it was very clear that he did not want to be with me. It was his woman friend who had brought him in — perhaps dragged would be a more appropriate word. I had already known her a long time. She had come in first and was sitting down, at ease. He followed reluctantly after and hovered at the door, not quite knowing what to do with himself. Eventually he perched himself with obvious discomfort between the woman and the door. The woman immediately began to speak, talking about him, talking about why they had come in together, but I interrupted her. I turned to the man and asked him to speak for himself. To begin with, did he want to be here? No, he said, he didn't want to be here. He didn't believe much in this kind of stuff. He wouldn't have come at all if the woman hadn't wanted it so much. He smiled an ironic smile and said that it seemed a prerequisite for the relationship that he be here, so he didn't have much option. He had fallen in love with the woman and wanted it to work out. He told me all this slowly, deliberately, as if considering every word carefully in advance, checking out each separate statement for its accuracy before committing it to the open air.

I then asked him, quite casually, to tell me something about himself, anything about his life that just happened to come to him in that moment. He hesitated, as if expecting a trap, then said there wasn't much of interest to tell really. He didn't remember much, but what he did remember was pretty boring. In the same logical tone he gave information about being an only boy of older parents and how he had spent a great deal of his early years alone trying to find things to do to occupy his time. Like what? He looked at me with those eyes that weren't quite as distant anymore. There was anger in them now. The more I asked him questions, the more resentful they became, defending territory that was clearly no concern of mine. It was obvious there was no space, no permission in this room for him. This was her space, not his, even though she was quietly sitting over on the other side of the room not saying a word. There was a long, heavy silence. Not a sound in the room. Nobody moved. The man and I sat looking at one another. Without my knowing how, our dialogue had turned into a confrontation, a power struggle. I felt locked into a situation from which I could not back down. His territory now, not mine. Impasse.

Yet still I repeated the question, dropping ever so slightly into a softer tone. Like what? He said again that there was nothing much, nothing he could really bring to mind. More silence. A sudden sharp pain across my chest. Then out of nowhere his eyes softened. They softened dramatically. The beginning of tears rose up into them, challenging the recent anger. The tears did not fall; they just stayed there in his eyes and washed the hardness away. For the first time he looked down. The confrontation was over. After a long pause, he spoke again. Despite the depth of feeling that had come into his eyes his voice held the same ordered, logical tone. Once, he said quietly, he had put a litter of kittens into a sack and beaten *them against the ground until they were all dead. As he said this, a terrible sadness came creeping across the logic of his tone. He hadn't thought about the incident for years, he added, and couldn't imagine what had made him think of it now. A slight pause. He felt ashamed, he said, for ever having thought of doing such an awful thing. He waited for a while before he raised his eyes again to meet mine. By the time they did they were guarded again, and the tears had gone back down. His eyes were now tinged with fear–fear of judgment, fear of being condemned. But before I could say anything, he had already changed the subject. I don't remember what he changed it to. It was something funny and he was laughing. I searched his face as the sharp jaw-line returned and wondered how such stunning softness had ever taken it over.*

(III)

Two people with acute sensitivity: the one almost inaccessible, the other in unimaginable pain. I used to think that some people were more sensitive than others; but after witnessing in astonishment the layers of many people falling away, I do not hold to that premise anymore. At core the fragility and richness are equal. The difference lies in the individual response when the sensitivity is assaulted. There are some who find a way to protect themselves under assault and so live, in a deadened state, far away from what their sensitivity has to offer them; and there are some who never find a way to protect themselves and live in a frenzied state, with their sensitivity constantly screaming in their ears. Neither of these states allows for the possibility of expansion because the place from which expansion begins has been seriously shaken. The original sensitive nature has either been safely shut away from the daily activity of life, or it has become an overwhelming adversary seriously doubting the possibility of survival itself.

Whether this nature is inaccessible or overexposed, faith in its efficacy has to be restored; for without its support the journey of self-discovery cannot get underway. The sensitive nature is the receiver for all that is alive. It registers the delicate differences between human beings, and only when a strong relationship with it is re-established can the subtle variations of that independent force make themselves known. This relationship has suffered a great deal, stirring up all manner of doubts and fears about whether life can be lived in a full way. It is for this reason that the initial movement towards self, the journey into the dark, can be so terrifying. It involves, finally, facing up to a central core of the being that has been reduced to a quivering mass by the insensitivity of others. On first contact it is only capable of sending out confused, indecipherable messages of alarm and will not, except under a great deal of encouragement, show off its resourceful side. The pain of what it has had to endure must be conveyed first.

This pain can be inflicted in any number of ways. In fact the deepest pain is often the most unexpected and unplaceable of all. What is a devastating experience for one person may be of no consequence to another. A person may be appalled at what is going on and at the same time observe others in the vicinity who remain quite unaffected because they do not engage perceptively in the same way. This was what happened to the two year old girl I have just described. Her sensitivity was wide open at this age and her perceptive powers working on many levels simultaneously, picking up details that were particular only to her mode of engagement with the outside world. This mode embraced a whole quality of experience that was altogether different from the rest of the family. She wanted to share it with them, but received no validation for what she felt and saw. This difference might have emerged unharmed even so, if she had been allowed the freedom to experience things in her own way and express herself in her own style. But something in the way she expressed herself, who knows what, disturbed her father deeply. Because of his own limitations he was not able to deal with his daughter's responses and so had to put a stop to it all. Yet since the girl was doing nothing overtly wrong, he could not bring himself to interfere in an obvious way. He could not justify to himself a direct form of punishment. So he engaged in what can only be described as a psychic power struggle with her. He found a way, without using voice or physical gesture, to terrify her. It had something to do with the expression on his face, but the power with which he affected the girl indicates much more than that. He literally stopped her in her tracks, not only taking away the beauty of what she saw, but loading her with the kind of fear that continued to invade her for years to come. Much of this power rested on the fact that she loved him and he, at other times, was able to express genuine love for her. She therefore became dependent on him as the only person who was able to give her some line of connection from the heart. She was not connected to her mother in this way at all. There was a lot of hate there, particularly because her mother refused to protect her when she was under her father's darker influence. But such hating was something quite clear compared to this kind of tortuous confusion. The depth of her connection with the father gave him energetic access to her that was powerful enough to destroy, and the openness of her sensitivity meant that she had no means of warding him off. Everything was locked in between them. None of the other children were affected by their father in this way and so it remained, for her, an inexplicable phenomenon for which she took all the blame. Before very long, she truly believed that she was a crazy child, and because of the secret stress, took on what everyone around her interpreted as crazy behavior. Given all this, it was not surprising that she made every effort, from then on, to bury the extraordinary visions she had once been so entranced by.

Helping her to recontact these visions and separate them from all the distortions that had developed along the way was a fascinating experience. Each time we returned to that moment when ecstasy gave way to fear, more details of the idiosyncratic nature of her seeing emerged. The way she originally enacted the behavior of her father was a first hint of this; she could not describe in words the dark, corkscrew energy that came at her, but had to rely on the power of gesture and emotions to take their place. To be with her in that intensely aware mode was to understand the limited function of language in her world as well as the numerous other channels of her experience. It was like learning a new and highly original form of communication. Yet at the same time it was easy to understand because so much was conveyed by the aliveness of her senses and the quick-changing expressions on her face. She was susceptible to a whole host of sensory impressions that, once given affirmation, fed her as no other food could have fed her, transmitting to her being an enthusiastic lightness of energy that leapt to the surface out of years of struggle and strain. Slowly this original language was able to filter back up from the two-year-old to the woman, suggesting that it was not too late to put it into operation again, that it could support her and give her a fullness of life again as it had then.

It was hard for her to understand that this sensory language could be of value to her present adult life. Her memory only reminded her of distancing looks and hostile responses; so it was a stretch for her to imagine anything differently, a stretch for her to recognize how completely she had eliminated the idea of true kinship. It was like a leap into the void with no guarantee that other people existed who had a similar degree of sensitivity and might accept her in her natural state as sane. The risk was one of trading her insanity for the insanity of others. The challenge was to embody her eccentricity fully, regardless of the reactions of those around her.

The original sensitivity, by telling of its pain, reopened itself to a world of wonder. Her father had deprived her of a great deal, had interrupted a chain of becoming at a time when life had hardly begun. He had interfered with an instinctive desire to create what had never been created before, to weave an individual design out of the experience of being alive. It was the beginning of this creative process that she was describing so vividly during our dialogue together: the child, her sensitive nature wide open, allowing her perceptions to play freely on the discoveries of her daily life, mixing the sensitive and the creative within herself so that the creator within her could be born.

(IV)

Sensitivity, as it becomes more finely tuned, aligns itself naturally and effortlessly with the creative force. But if it is interfered with and forced to close down, it boils with anger inside, becoming an agent that wants to destroy. The boy with the sack of kittens is an obvious example.

The saddest part of my meeting with him was being unable to reach to the appalling things that were done to him before he found such a brutal outlet of revenge. The fact that he told me about what he had done was amazing enough in its own way, but I was reluctant to accept what I immediately knew to be true: that what was done to him first would, most likely, never reach the light of day. He is a shy, gentle, very loving man. I found that out afterwards very gradually, hour by hour, as he let himself be known to me in his own time. What I had encountered on first meeting was his well-practiced style of protection, one that he had developed as defense against the alarming gentleness he had felt as a child. What happened to this gentleness must have been severe indeed because one day he found himself pounding a litter of kittens to death in wild rage at what had been done, and clearly was still being done, to him. There could be no other explanation for such an unwarranted act of violence from a boy with such an underlying gentleness of heart. He must have learned this violence from someone else, and only the acuteness of his own experience could have presented him with the appropriate model for this action. He had declared war on kittens, the most helpless of all creatures, because only they, I presume, represented accurately the helplessness of his own plight. He had to make sure he won in exact proportion to the degree he had lost on previous occasions and so take on at least some semblance of power. It is not a large step to see the kittens as representatives of the boy's sensitivity. He was playing out the death of his most fragile part, playing out in a frenzy what it felt like to have his own gentleness beaten out of him.

The wider implications of this incident are sobering indeed, more troubling, certainly, than the woman's terrorized life, however extreme that may have been. If there is one advantage for those whose sensitivity remains hyper-alive inside of them, it is that the destructive backlash is unlikely to occur. As constant recipients of the power of destruction they are reluctant to play out that destruction towards others, because they are only too aware of the extent of its harm. But those who have left their sensitivity behind have also left behind the memory of being destroyed, and whatever they do in response will be done without an awareness of where it came from or what the dynamics are that propel them into action. For me it is relatively easy to offer welcome to a sensitive nature that has been pulled apart at the seams and is obvious in its distress. I only have to give it sufficient space to circulate in all its chaos and discordancy. It may take a while and decide to fling itself in many different directions now that sufficient safety is guaranteed, but eventually it will play itself out and begin to align itself accordingly. However, to offer welcome to a sensitive nature before it has made a clear decision to re-emerge is a delicate and more difficult notion. There is no hint of what its identity might be and no guarantee that it will ever decide to reveal the degree of its pain. Hence my surprise at the flash of that sudden opening through which appeared the stark picture of a furious boy—not only the violence of it, but the underlevel of shame that put into motion the possibility of release from the whole affair.

With this kind of hidden sensitivity there is a particularly subtle dynamic at work, engaging me in a continuous, almost unconscious, search for the kind of opening he gave. When this man first came into the room, a part of me closed down. I was not aware of this when it happened, but became conscious of it by the time we were locked in confrontation and my questions began to take on for him an interrogative tone. At that point I caught what was happening, deliberately softening my tone when I asked "like what?" for the second time. I do not know how much difference that slight alteration of tone had on him; the essential thing is that I myself became conscious of being closed. This awareness gave me the chance to shift the energy and open up channels of communication that had so far been unavailable to us. For in these situations the only reliable foundation I have to stand on is my own sensitive nature. If I do not provide an opening for my own to come through, I cannot expect his in return; what is more, I have to find a way to transmit my sensitivity energetically to him, transmit even the pain of my own wounding, if it is in any way part of the present dynamic between us.

The experience of recovering my own sensitivity has taught me that the layers around it can be endless. So much so that I have given up imagining an end to the process of peeling them all away. In my most intense moments of awareness these layers feel like steel bands, and as the bands loosen their grip on me one by one, I am left each time as raw and defenseless as the last. My shock at each stage of exposure never diminishes, neither does my surprise at the tenacity of each line of defense, at how guarded I still continue to be. So when I am with someone like this man, I remain acutely conscious of the gradual nature of the process and the degree of protection required if any of those steel bands are going to come off at all. Only by taking responsibility for how open I am at any given time can any worthwhile exchange get underway. When the sensitivity is already accessible to me, as it was with the woman, I become the follower. She leads me into her own world of specialized perceptions and communications. She shows me around and lets me know who she is. But if there is no initial access, I have to become the leader through the unspoken medium of my own openness. There is no path to follow then but my own.

(V)

Because I have used examples of this man and this woman in such opposing terms, it would be easy to conclude that this is a normal pattern of male/female response. Nothing would be further from the truth. If I had felt so inclined, I could have readily reversed the situation and presented a woman out of touch with her own sensitive nature and a man overwhelmed by his. Even though it seems more common for a boy to distance himself from his own nature during childhood, I have been with many examples of men whose veneer of defense is thin and frighteningly raw once the sensitized environment has had a chance to filter through. In fact, to reach the sensitive vein is to open up a place that does not take into account any kind of sexual separation. Therein lies the pleasure and richness of the discovery. Instead of making divisions, it brings together all creative potential into one mass melting pot. Each individual, whether male or female, can draw from it whatever inspiration or expression is desired. Divisions and limitations are arbitrarily imposed at an early age and the blocked imagination cannot initially grasp how they can ever come together again into a single stream. All in all, the sensitive nature does not deal well with forms unless they are of its own making, and it will not cooperate until those that do not fit are swept away for the shaping impulse to start all over again.

When sensitivity meets with sensitivity, the potential for true closeness can begin. If its balance and identity can be found individually, then the ground is prepared for meetings between people that can reach a very deep level indeed. If sensitivities, open to an equal degree but distinct in their individual identity, develop on both sides, then relating becomes a delicate interchange through which many different qualities of energy are brought into play. At the heart of this intimacy is a merging in which all distinctions fall away and the sensitivities find their common source. But between this merging and the first casual meeting there is an infinite range of contact, a testing process so that the sensitivities make sure they are going to be met in a manner that is for their own good. The more the sensitivities find their aliveness and become confident in their unique modes of perception, the more they will be able to choose, from the many alternatives available, how they want to engage.

This closeness has many forms, not all of which are connected to fellow human beings. A very large older man from Texas, with cowboy boots and a long, loping stride has been coming to see me for quite some time. Despite his imposing bulk, his full, deep voice and the anger that periodically boils up from under his eyes, he has the look inside of someone who has been subjected to severe emotional assault for the greater part of his life. Very gradually I found out that it had become a habit for him to keep slamming his sensitivity against a brick wall. It had been frighteningly alive in an unsympathetic setting when he was a child and beaten to a pulp. Now all he could do was keep beating his sensitive nature down himself in case it came too strongly back to life. This brick wall took on a number of forms, not least of which was a series of failed relationships with women. The result was always the same: a numbed out sensitivity and no space taken between relationships to recover and look around at life from his own independent and acutely sensitive vantage point. His sensitivity had always existed but never been of service to him, bandied around as it had been in conflict with one woman after another before he was able to find out how to keep it and treasure it for himself. For the past two years there has been no woman in his life. This is a new experience for him, a difficult and puzzling one, at times almost impossible because of the loneliness he has to sustain. Then a few weeks ago he brought in something he had written. The writing consisted of two delicate vignettes describing in loving, poetic detail an egret fishing by the ocean shore and a red-headed girl running and playing in the sun. Almost as an afterthought he included a final paragraph. In it he acknowledged that for sixty years his life had all but passed him by, and now finally, he was allowing himself time to look around and find out how much of it he has been missing.

•

XII. INNOCENCE AND REALITY

Now for the grounding.

Sensitivity, particularly when it makes an appearance after a long absence, feels like mush. It appears to have no substance, no shape, no capacity to deal with everyday life. Furthermore, it activates all kinds of extreme feelings and can leave a person immersed in them for a long period of time without direction or relief. It is not surprising there is a reluctance to make contact again.

This mush, however, is not the sensitivity's original state of being. Rather, it is a record of much pain, the result of being smashed around and denied free participation in the living process. The sensitive nature is a deeply feeling center as well as a delicate instrument of awareness that has been thrown out of alignment. As a consequence, it emits confused signals in a continuous urge to realign, to rediscover the coherent pattern of its existence.

But the coherence of this pattern cannot be re-established without the truth. And the truth can only enter through an unmasking of those relationships that contributed to the sensitivity's mushed state. This is a truth that has been left behind a long time ago because the child was not strong enough to fight for it or claim it from the beginning as its own. Nevertheless the sensitive nature has never entirely given up. In its own haphazard, injured way, it has remained on the alert, hoping for some return signal, for some possibility of realignment with a reality it still adheres to despite misconceptions of the past.

As soon as even one return signal is picked up, then all energy is directed towards aligning with it and attempting to make the connection that will contribute to its own recovery. Once this initial contact is made, the mush begins to take on some kind of substance and shape. Furthermore, the sensitivity can gradually let go of the pain and focus on restoring its true identity.

Only truth can create this grounding, no matter how strange or unexpected it may turn out to be. It is essential to return to the past not with the purpose of taking up residence there, but so as to get the facts and the feelings straight.

(II)

Some children are connected to their parents and some are not. And when I say connected, I mean truly connected with a bond that is deep. Obviously all children are connected to their parents in some way because they are dependent on them for a very basic kind of survival. They have to be fed, housed, clothed and cared for and somebody has to do it for them. But this need for survival does not necessarily mean a deep connection, one that tugs at the heartstrings and promotes a strong desire to know one another, human being to human being. The need for survival does not guarantee the existence of love. In fact confusion between the two is what begins the masking of those early relationships, begins the illusion in the parent, as well as the child, that a deeper connection exists when in fact it does not.

The mother gives birth to the child and for that very reason believes she ought to love it deeply. Yet she may find out very soon, on a level that has nothing to do with the expectations of mother and child, that the nature of this young person she has given birth to is not at all to her liking. There may be all sorts of complicated reasons, such as environment or timing, for why this liking is unable to surface, but the result is still the same. She may continue to feed, house and clothe the child, but is still not attracted to the being she has given birth to and that is the truth.

The child feels the energy of the mother who is feeding it and is uncomfortable—ill at ease, perhaps, with the rhythm of her movements or jarred by the tone of her voice. Maybe there is an anxiety within the mother that makes ease and relaxation impossible. Whatever the cause, the child does not feel welcome, even though the basic requirements are met and needs filled that are essential to survival. Yet despite the fact that these needs are filled in a basic way, the child continues to feel more and more of a stranger to the mother. It does not like her and that is also the truth.

Within this situation there is already a relationship forming. It is not a relationship that offers much sustenance and for that reason will not be easy to deal with; but it is the reality of these particular beings placed in each other's proximity for the first time. However, because of the expectations of the mother/child relationship, there is little room for the reality of this dynamic to be assimilated and accepted for what it is. Somewhere, fighting the reality, lies an insistence that the situation ought to be different: the mother should love the child and the child the mother. It is a fixed concept, set up in advance before the true character of the relationship even begins, and the rigidity of that concept prevents consideration of the infinite number of variations that naturally offer themselves in the forming of any new relationship. Caught between the ideal set up in advance and the reality of how these two people actually feel about each other, the relationship is already in struggle, already working against the grain of its true nature, already losing its grounding in reality.

From this point all sorts of difficult questions arise. If there is not much feeling attraction on either side, how can the child ensure its own survival needs without involving itself in some pretense of loving? How can it distinguish between the survival and the loving, and accept that this separation exists and always will? And, to extend the scenario further, what if the father comes on the scene, or even someone quite unconnected to the family, and fills the need for deep contact that could not be satisfied through the mother? Can room be given for that relationship to develop in its unique way? Can full acknowledgement ever be given to the true nature of these various relationships, even though they demand a serious adjustment to all the pre-fabricated family roles?

The disintegration of the nuclear family that is happening at this time is not caused by the idea of family **per se**. Rather it is being strangled by the rigid, repetitive structure that has been gathered around it, a rigidity that does not allow the truth of relationships to develop in their own time. There is one allowable pattern and one only; and if things do not fit into that pattern, they are forced out of their original shape until they do. Thus there is little room for true intimacy to form, or for individuals to break free and seek out the deeper connections they need.

When this kind of flexibility is not possible, when the truth of these early relationships cannot be established outside the rigid rules of what a family ought to be, then long-lasting complications ensue. Individuals come of age and find out, often with somewhat of a shock, that the real relationships to their parents are quite different from what they had imagined. The distortion that begins in childhood grows increasingly extreme, and the gap between the real and the fictional relationships ever wider. This continues until the sensitivity can no longer put up with the split and has to make a mammoth return to recover its lost foundations. And the only reason a person has to return so far into the past is because the ability to connect was thrown into confusion so early.

(III)

To have no true connection with either parent is a particularly agonizing experience, particularly behind the closed doors of the average nuclear family. I am thinking of one particular girl who identified herself early in her life as an orphan, and who indeed might have found more nurturing for herself had she actually been one and searched out another family to take her under their care. She was smart enough to figure out her mother right away and having done so, did her best to keep as much distance from her as she could. This does not mean that she was not constantly wary of her when she was in her presence, but she had no illusions about the neglect and hostility that came her way. At a surprisingly early age she recognized that her mother was far too emotionally confused to offer her any kind of support and resigned herself to its perpetual absence. In fact, at certain crucial stages of her childhood, she was able to find substitute nurturing in the mothers of her friends and so, from a state of starvation, satisfied a minimum of maternal requirement. But she could not reject her father in the same way, even though his hostility and neglect were equally extreme. It is likely that there was a moment of connection with him when she was a baby, a brief period of time when some direct loving did find its way through; but he was already putting her down for her excessive energy by the time she was two. He then left for the Korean war and returned six months later a very changed man. From the moment of his return he exhibited no affection towards her or the rest of the family, offering little more than harsh judgments and self-absorbed monologues during the short times he was at home.

But the girl could not give up on him. Either she could not lay down the memory of that brief early contact or she was simply desperate for some kind of attention, some slight gesture of approval, some signal of warmth that would show her that she had not been discarded completely. But of course this only made the situation worse. The more desperate the attempts, the harsher the rejections, her self-esteem continuing to plummet year by year. It is interesting that no nurturing substitutes appeared to fill the father's role as they did the mother's, and the reason for this is obvious. There was no space for them to come in. Despite overwhelming evidence to the contrary, hope was still invested in the father; the fantasy still remained alive that one day he would stop, turn around, and acknowledge her for the extraordinary child that she was underneath so much inhibition and shame.

The girl was then faced, at the age of eleven, with what would seem from the outside to be a very difficult decision imposed on an already difficult enough life. Her parents split up and she was given the freedom to decide which one of them she wanted to live with. But for the child the decision was not difficult at all. Without hesitation she chose her father, truly believing that now, finally, she would have him to herself and all would be well between them. Yet he continued to ignore her in the same way as before; in fact even more pointedly because there were only the two of them and the responsibilities of the family did not provide a cover anymore. The hostility was directed towards her and her alone. She had to argue with him for the smallest amount of money to buy the most basic requirements of food and clothing; otherwise there was literally no contact, and so much shame had built up around him by this time that she never even considered the possibility of bringing any of her friends back to spend time with her. Most important of all, on the deepest level she still had not given up on him. She left his house as soon as she could get a job to support herself and, not many years later, met a man with the same tease of possible connection and the same determination to continually put her down. She stayed married to him for twenty years, still believing that the man's love and approval would eventually come her way.

There is a heart-breaking wastage of energy in this kind of illusion, not to speak of its complex, long-term reverberations. Once it comes to be directed so exclusively, once illusion enters as the final emergency measure to divert the terror of abandonment, it holds on for dear life. It will not loosen its grip because it is the last resort. Obsession takes over and closes the imagination to any other alternatives. It is simple enough, from an objective perspective, to identify the ludicrous nature of this obsession, even to ridicule such a bizarre, single-minded desire for someone who has never for one moment shown himself to be on the child's side. The lack of support has been proven again and again through direct experience. But for the girl-become-woman it is very far from simple. It is the most exacting challenge of all to move from that obsession, to give up on that single road to survival and acknowledge that, no matter how much energy is expended in that direction, it will always lead to a dead end.

(IV)

The quality that takes hold most fiercely in a situation like this is a remarkably stubborn form of innocence. This innocence is the obsession's staunchest ally and in the recovery process turns out to be the most formidable opponent of all. Innocence is fine as long as the child finds the early connection that leads to being deeply fed and sustained. Ideally the child should be able to luxuriate in this natural form of innocence, confident that an unlimited supply of safety and love will always be there. The outside world can then be dealt with little by little accordingly. An unhurried period of adjustment is allowed for, and the love remains as a constant source of energy to return to in case the impact of the real world becomes too harsh or too strong.

But if that deep early connection is not there, another quality of innocence comes into being that acts not as support, but as a form of deception. Its intention is to give support, but on an inner level it does not work out that way. For this particular quality of innocence is formed out of desperation, and it is based on a refusal to believe the extent of suffering going on. The first priority for any child is to find a loving connection; if it is not found, the child has to find a way to convince itself otherwise. To accept the reality of no connection is too much to bear and is the equivalent of being doomed before the struggle of living has even begun. For this reason the innocence has to hold hard and fast to its false claim. The protective instincts move into emergency mode and reject the version of reality they are presented with. They begin transforming the people around them by finding some excuse for their behavior, some reason why they are going about their lives in such a hurtful and unpredictable way. As soon as this protective process begins, the child is no longer on its own side. On the contrary, it has abandoned its own plight and allied itself with the insensitivity that is the cause of its pain. Then in response to this abandonment the sensitivity, with its natural instinct for the truth, begins to lose its clarity and its command. It cannot any longer support the child as it would like to do, cannot remain active for the child's good in the face of so much confusing information.

Yet there is still more confusion to come because the sensitivity, in its weakened state, goes on trying. Ousted from its most supportive role, it takes on another. It takes on the role of justifier rather than truth-teller, hoping that this shift will save the day. Since it has already been forbidden to acknowledge the truth, it learns how to bypass the unattractive surface behavior of people and move behind in search of their more kindly qualities, even though those qualities remain hidden for most of the time and seldom engage in the process of day-to-day communication. The sensitivity, if successful in the search, then convinces itself that these hidden qualities represent far more accurately who these individuals really are. At the same time the cruelty suffered from them is laid aside as untrue.

This search process involves a deep form of insight that is in itself a natural attribute, so the sensitive nature does not take long to perfect this justifying role. All that is required is for the harsher side of life to be completely separated off from the more loving side. The one, the overt behavior, is discarded as if it did not exist, while the other, the hidden essence, is given total focus as if it were continually visible for the whole world to see. And if this hidden part does, by any chance, become visible for a moment, any sign of good behavior is instantly seized upon as incontrovertible evidence that this version of reality is true. Every surfacing of potentially supportive qualities, however infrequent, extends the life of this mythical version and prolongs the agony of the child.

For by now the agony is intense. A part of the child feels this acutely, but the more active part is frantically staving it off, pretending that its suffering is not that extreme and probing ever deeper for those redeeming qualities that it knows lurks in the furthest recesses of every human being. As it probes, it is all the time being battered, but the probing mission is so obsessive that the battering is scarcely ever acknowledged for the intense punishment it is meting out. The agony comes as much from the ever-widening split in the child's consciousness, the compulsive over-working of the sensitive vein, as it does from the loneliness of feeling separate, of not being acknowledged or seen.

If a child's sensitivity has not been interfered with, it will learn in its own time how to distinguish between what is in its favor and what is not. It is designed to make exactly those distinctions. From the beginning it has been aware of all the layers of consciousness operating in other people and will know whether they are sufficiently integrated to provide a safe harbor. At birth it finds a trust that can be fully relied on and so, from the simple process of comparison, will learn to recognize a situation that does not contain that trust. But if there is no trust in the first place, survival energy will move in fast and the innocence will become confused. The accurate information transmitted is that all situations are untrustworthy. It acts on that information, but at the same time is instinctively looking for something more secure. So badly does it want contact of a nurturing kind that it will keep looking for signs of trust everywhere. But by this time anything like a balanced perspective has gone, and the child is likely to be fooled by any resemblance to the real thing, continuing later on in life to create relationships that merely perpetuate the original insatiable desire.

On all accounts this is a no-win situation. These people have no way of confronting the harsher side of life because they keep insisting that it does not exist. Yet these are the very people who become the most helpless victims of the harsher side, who, when they find themselves in punishing situations, still swear on their innocence to protect them. By this time they are firmly on the side of their punishers anyway and have no means of returning to themselves. The truth is they hardly know anymore that there is a self to return to, so beaten about has it been and deemed worthless in everyone's eyes.

So for any change to happen, for the grounding to come in and give the sensitivity some foundation, it is the innocence that has to be broken. Only then can a passage be cleared back to the child's side, back to the original power that is very far from innocent and very far from the soft-spoken protector of people it has convinced itself to be.

(V)

As this innocence disintegrates, my role is to form a bridge between very opposite worlds. I have to hold up both sides so that the crossing from illusion to reality can be safely made. First of all I find entry into the innocent side and fully absorb the desperate straits of the person who has championed it. On this side of the bridge there is seldom much coherence of communication once the surface is exposed. Most of this confusion can only be expressed on a feeling level because out of the chaos little logical sense remains. There is no order to life on a deeper level, for all the parts that made up that inner depth have become separated. Nothing connects to anything else; the design has no flow. What does remain, however, despite the jumble, is a remarkably original perception about things. It surfaces in flashes amid the confusion, something that might at first seem like flights of fancy, bizarre ways of looking at people, odd notions about things. This is the turbulent underside, covered over by this stubborn innocence and only re-exposed when a full measure of safety is felt again. On the immediate surface, before any deeper exploration begins, there may be little visible disturbance: an everyday life well managed and well under control. There has certainly been enough survival practice to perfect this coping ability, and along with it, there remains a surprising strength of will, no matter how painful the underside that is being endured. It might even appear that this will power could continue in survival mode indefinitely, continuing to deceive all and sundry with its surface calm, had it not been reminded of the difference between survival and loving, between making do and coming fully alive.

So there is, on the one hand, this will, combined with an acute sensory awareness and an uncanny gift of knowing: signs that the sensitivity and the truth have not entirely given up on their desire to re-align with one another. On the other hand there is this innocence that continues to foul everything up, protecting me and everyone else from the intense and ruthless perceptions that seethe silently on the underside. The mouth wants to open and make unspeakable pronouncements about all sorts of things, but the innocence cuts it off before it can begin to let the words and sounds go. The one side hints at being all-knowing while the other professes a dismal ignorance, and they shuttle back and forth in confusion, all their energy taken up with reinterpreting and modifying the disturbing reality around them.

The ingenuity of this radar operation is endless, but it cannot be switched off or turned inwards because the pain of the ensuing discoveries would be too much. It is a whole lot easier to protect others, and by doing so remain innocent, than own up to and deal with the cruelty that has pursued these beings through the twisted labyrinths of their own lives. So they cut themselves off from their own brilliance and drift disconnected until they can find someone else who is willing to cross over and join them, both in their brilliance and in the misery that comes from keeping that brilliance hidden away.

If this joining is complete on an emotional and energetic level, then the innocence will lose its hold surprisingly fast. It has only been pushed to such an extreme to make the loneliness bearable, to fabricate some semblance of company while the dearth goes on. Its function had been to mute and soften everything, to blend everything into an indistinguishable haze so that the sharpness of the pain is dulled and the fine details of such a harsh reality denied. The loneliness is certainly a deep one, but it only has to be touched at that depth by another's silent knowing for its own knowing to recover a sense of confidence again. Its memory is quick and long.

This touch, this joining has a lot of power. It provokes violent shock and utter relief at the same time. It is another instance of death and birth coming together: the death of innocence and the birth of a possibly appalling reality existing side by side with equal parts of terror and exhilaration to balance them. And within this paradox there is bewilderment also, for what has previously been a warning of destruction now offers, at the same time, the physical sensation of a new kind of power, a feeling of the self merging with its own reality rather than keeping it constantly at bay. The former destroyer of the self thus offers its creative foundations for the first time.

It is at this moment of the sensitivity's grounding that the original explorer returns. For a while fascination and repulsion hang in the balance as the first details of a new reality find their way home. But fascination is already, at this stage, gaining the upper hand because it is backed by a curiosity about life's unknown that is hard to put down. Furthermore, the sensitive nature can take a surprising number of shocks once judgement has been withdrawn and the protective innocence is no longer required. The way is open for self-inquiry to take its course and direct inward, rather than outward, its formidable powers of knowing. There is no lack of perception here; and as the sensitivity, instead of manipulating the lives of others, begins to rediscover its own center, much beauty comes to the surface that went unnoticed before. It is remarkable how thoroughly the beautiful aspects are denied while survival is the primary concern. As if beauty in the self requires its own form of peaceful witnessing which the urgency of survival does not allow. In a sense, the emergency form of innocence casts the extremes of both ugliness and beauty to one side, limiting the range of expression to a narrow middle ground. And to take one's life back is to draw in with it all those excesses of behavior that were eliminated in the single-minded determination to find a way through.

So this is the mush become substance. The sensitivity finds identity so that it can move into action again, finds energy so that it can move towards passion again, and finds ruthlessness, if need be, so that it can move towards the harsher realities it has been avoiding. For the justifier to give over to the truth-teller is a radical shift, for it means championing the self rather than championing others. A complete change of sides is involved that may not be welcomed by some of those so-called friends who have been protecting themselves under the shelter of this soft-mouthed innocence. Little of the truth has been ventured in the past and much more will need to be declared as the present and the self grow larger and the distortions of the old reality fall away. Sometimes it means a falling away of much that seemed of value in the past. But what looks like loss on the outside turns out to be gain on the inside: nothing less than vital energy reclaimed and returned to its rightful owner, its rightful place. •

XIII. RELEASING THE FOOL

A four year old girl was eating cherries from a tree in the back garden of her home. It was one of her favorite things to do, to escape into the garden alone, climb high up into the tree and reach for the brightly colored clusters hanging thickly from the branches. Nobody could see her from the house, and she could eat as much of the sweet fruit as she wanted. The tree had always been her own kingdom anyway, safe from all intruders. Then something terrible happened that had never happened before. She swallowed a cherry whole, pit and all. Instantly all her joy was gone, and her body tightened with fear. She sat there on the branch, unable to move, the fear growing inside. Then a rush of panic drove her into action. She scrambled down the tree, bruising her knees, almost falling several times, and rushed headlong into the house. She had to find someone quick, before it was too late. She ran into the living-room to discover her mother sitting around with a group of her women friends. She stood there breathless, unable to make a sound.

"What is it, Barbara?" her mother asked. "I'm busy right now."

Still the fear gripped her, and she could not open her mouth to speak. Her mother repeated the question. She was annoyed. She did not like to be interrupted, particularly when her friends were around. At last she found some words. "I was eating cherries in the garden and...and..." She began to cry, trying desperately to hold back the tears.

"What, Barbara? What are you trying to say? I told you I was busy." Her mother did not move and her voice was harder than before.

She could not hold the tears back anymore. They came all at once in a burst and she cried out, sobbing, "I ate one of the stones. I ate the cherry and the stone as well."

"Pull yourself together, Barbara. There's nothing wrong in that.

What are you so upset about?"

"But...but..." Sobbing more and more despairingly. "A cherry tree is going to grow inside me and I'll die." She had finally been able to say it. Now they would understand and do something. But was there really anything they could do to help her, to save her? Surely it was already too late. And she cried even harder at the sheer hopelessness of it all. But not one of the women made a move towards her. Instead, to her hurt and astonishment, they burst out laughing. All of them were uproariously laughing. Through her tears she saw, like a nightmare, blurred, grotesque faces jeering at her and in her ears she heard a shrieking chaos of sound. Inside her and outside her everything was turning around. She wanted to disappear. She wanted the ground to swallow her whole. They were all looking at her and laughing. This terrible thing had happened; she was going to die, and they were all laughing. Somehow she managed to turn away, to find some movement in her legs again and run from the room, away from the horror of those faces and that awful sound. She ran back out into the garden, the sound still following in waves behind her. She tore past the cherry tree and plunged into the thick bushes against the fence at the far end. She lay there hidden, spread-eagle, her body shaking all over, her heart thumping frantically against the ground.

This is one story among many that have been told to me of children subjected to mockery, giving me to understand that being made a fool of is perhaps the deepest injury that the sensitive nature can sustain. Experiences such as these have an extraordinarily lasting impact, and the details remain in the memory for a long period of time. There is something about the humiliation of laughter that reaches to the core and leaves the injury trembling there, raw and inconsolable. When sensitivity is assaulted, a whole range of emotions run riot through the system; but mockery, I believe, is the source of them all. It is the great isolator, the experience that separates the child's reality from the reality of others, introducing for the first time the shadows of a world that could be insane.

In the scene I have just described a highly imaginative child is mocked outrageously by a thoughtless group of women. She is mocked only because she conceives of things differently, because she is alive to a larger range of possibility than those around her. She is at an age when the creative imagination is just beginning to flower, and as part of the flowering process she has to extend tentative lines of communication to the outside world. She needs gently to test these imaginings because, as they begin to emerge from deep within the self, they are often disturbing and some kind of reassurance is required. The more open the sensitive nature, the further the imagination will go and the greater the reassurance that is required. However, as this example shows, what often happens is the reverse: the richer the imagination, the more unlikely it is to be given any kind of acceptance. The more the child's version of reality deviates from what is considered normal, the more it opens itself to ridicule and scorn. Who knows how or when this girl first conceived of the possibility of a cherry tree growing inside of her body, but she was sufficiently convinced of its reality to anticipate nothing less than death as a result. Yet what was deadly serious to her became mere entertainment for her mother and her friends, not only exacerbating the fear, but leaving what she had imagined locked inside of her like an unreleased bad dream. On the other hand, with caring and attention of the right kind, it could have been released into something very different, transformed into something that the child herself might appreciate and enjoy, fertilizing the growing imagination even more. A story could have been made of it; in fact, anything could have been made of it other than this stigma of stupidity and humiliation, other than the hard edge of laughter that she will have to shun at all costs from now on.

(II)

The Fool is a major figure in almost every esoteric and literary tradition of the world. He is the one who takes a different course and, in so doing, brings the risk of mockery onto his head. In whatever tradition he appears, he is always a fascinating and complex character because he combines so many contradictory traits. He is at the same time foolish and wise, innocent and devious, crazy and sane, and sometimes it is difficult to distinguish which characteristic is manifesting at any given time. For example, the tradition of the Tarot has given the Fool card the number zero, thereby suggesting that he does not belong to the ordered, linear progression of the other cards. He has a life of his own, unplaceable, indefinable, yet containing within himself some aspect of all the other twenty-one cards. The idea has been carried on in the Joker of the regular deck, the wild card, the one that is different, that can change identity according to the game being played.

Of the many figures in literature that have been created from this tradition, perhaps the most strikingly and highly developed is the Fool in Shakespeare's *King Lear*. His overt role is as court jester to the King's retinue, a role that gives him permission to play the fool at will. It is his job to entertain in a theatrically improvised style and comment on the events in the kingdom as they develop day by day. In the situation of this play these events develop increasingly towards disaster. Through a series of rash decisions that lead to his own rejection and isolation, it is the King who shows himself to be the true fool. Meanwhile, through his role as jester, the Fool keeps trying to give the King insights into the stupidity of what he has done, keeps trying to show him how little he knows about himself, despite his long experience as leader of his kingdom. He not only becomes teacher to a man who seems incapable of receiving any kind of wisdom whatsoever; but he stays with him through all his hardships, ending up with him in a howling storm, still trying to find a way to bring home the truth. And his efforts are not entirely wasted, for the King becomes aware of many of his own failings before he dies. But the extremity of it all takes it toll and the Fool dies also. He dies for the sake of the truth, using his creative imagination to its fullest extent and committing himself to any extremes of behavior to ensure that a new sense of order is restored.

In this dramatization the Fool is the seer, the improviser and the creator, all in one. He gives himself permission to be as outlandish as he needs to be in the expression of his own knowing, and he cherishes his understanding that every aspect of human nature has its flip side. He also embodies a constant interweave of theater and life and never stays in one spot long enough to be caught by those who would want to pin him down.

(III)

On the surface the girl in the garden and this portrait of the Fool seem to have little in common with each other. Yet they are at source the same. They are both, in the eyes of the people around them, considered impossibly strange. They are singled out as individuals who think and speak in a different language, and because the way they express themselves does not tally with an accepted version of reality, they become obvious targets of scorn. The child, however, does not have the strength or confidence to deal with all this. She is too afraid of her own imagination and craves a supportive environment to deal with that fear and to expand on the ideas and images that are bursting up within her. She needs a catalyst through which she can begin to express all those zany elements that make up her unique vision and style. If she ends up having nothing and nobody to bounce off, she feels crazy, stupid and alone. It is with these negative feelings that the creative imagination associates itself from then on. Her potential contribution to life is cut short; she is of no value to others and so deems herself worthless all around.

Shakespeare, however, creates with remarkable insight a dramatic situation in which the girl can find her place and thrive. In his world the full flower of her seemingly crazy imagination is welcomed and given earth-changing powers. Shakespeare's Fool has to accept from the outset that the majority of the world will see him as crazy. He does what the girl is never encouraged to do, which is to take on the courage of his own difference and remain unaffected by the way people respond. He takes confidence in his own wisdom gathered through experience, and can recognize that the folly people assign to him really belongs to themselves. He is never acknowledged openly as truth-teller, but he does not have to be. The events of the play bear him out. As audience we are witness to the confidence of his chosen identity and understand how it is the only role that will lead him through so much falsity to the right course of action. We watch as he takes on a seemingly impossible task, yet little by little he ferrets out the truth, no matter how deeply it has been buried underground.

So the girl has to somehow open up a pathway towards the confidence of the Fool. There is no question that unless she finds the support she needs, unless she has opportunity to contact her wounded sensitivity again, she will continue to be haunted and blocked by the mockery of that scene. Yet the fool-child is the last identity she wants to return to. She is the one who always does things the wrong way or comes out with the least appropriate remarks at the worst possible time. She is the one who tries so hard to be the same as everyone else, tries so hard to figure out the way that everyone else does things so that she will not have that appalling laughter descending on her again. But she is who she is. She is different, no matter how anyone responds, and the difference will always be impossible to hide. She has to come up against the horror of that fool-child again and let her know that, with the sensitivity whole, there is a way that she can be fulfilled.

It is uncanny how many people who first come to see me expect, as a matter of course, to be laughed at. From the outset some of them have already switched to the mocking side and treat their own inner existence as a joke. They have become convinced that their way of looking at the world is crazy simply because so many people have derided it for so long. So they josh about themselves in a half-hearted fashion and that wildly imaginative part remains hidden away in silence, in shame. I have discovered by now that within this awkwardness a wealth of inventiveness lies. It is probable that nobody has ever been party to it and never will be until this sensitivity to ridicule is first soothed. Without assurance of protection from scorn, the imagination will not reveal anything of the magic it invariably contains. What it contains is strange indeed, fascinatingly strange, particularly as it is still groping for some form of connection that would make its imaginings whole. When first encouraged to come out, it is likely to stutter in fragments, still expecting the familiar mockery to cut it down. It is this difference that has always been mocked, yet it is the very same difference that is the seed of creativity waiting to be sown. The change begins only when this difference is honored; and as soon as the honoring begins, the fool-child can reappear in a very different guise from the child who was scorned.

The Fool is so deeply involved here because he is the one who honors all differences, no matter how bizarre they may initially seem. If his example were not around to contain them all, these differences would want to slide back into the shadows again and so lose their life and color once and for all. So as it emerges, the original spirit has to be given room to spread. These extreme tendencies have to find a still greater extremity if need be; anything rather than be pulled back into the lines of conformity that have been so harshly represented by those mocking tones. Foundations have to be created to strengthen those differences, to give them full power over their unpredictable nature and form. It is hard for people to accept that what they have been mocked for is actually their greatest strength. Because of so much ridicule in the past, there is still a deeply engrained pressure to conform, which gives them no option but to abandon altogether the fool's identity that has already caused them so much pain. What the long tradition of the Fool teaches, however, is to stay with integrity amid a tangle of deceit and to follow the truth to its ultimate extreme. His eccentricities, deeply rooted inside, are his only integrity. With no model to follow, he can only follow his own idiosyncratic way, learning how to improvise through every situation as best he can and discovering how the false masks of others inevitably fall away.

(IV)

The Fool in us needs to find confidence because only then can his wisdom come through. Those who are subject to mockery at an early age are often laughed at simply because they have a deeper insight into what happens around them. They tend to see what others would rather they did not see. To be able to see too much too early is a truly uncomfortable fate for a child because so much energy comes flying back to block it, to jeer at it, to label it as inappropriate and weird. A child who sees and feels the truth takes on a dangerous occupation, and indeed the danger of it does not change. It is there for life and will continue until the truth becomes a more acceptable attribute. What can change is physical size and a growing confidence in the wisdom that is stored in every human soul. Then the responses of others will not matter so much. Besides, it is only the child's doubt that opens the door to mockery in the first place, a doubt that rapidly escalates into fear as soon as the severity of the attack is thrust home.

As the confidence grows and wisdom moves back in, another lost element returns also, almost of its own accord. Children who are ridiculed lose their own sense of humor very soon. They become a target for humor before they have a chance to develop their own comic style. However, once the threat of mockery dissipates, it soon becomes evident that this over-serious demeanor is associated with fear, with a constant wariness, not with a lack of comic flare. Humor was always meant to act as a natural ally to insight, and it is surprising how easily they come together again once the sensitivity returns. The joke is no longer directed inward on the self, but expands outward from the being in appreciation of the cosmic humor of the world. Theater and life begin to play with each other, moving in and out at will and redirecting the insistence of other people's scorn.

People use mockery mostly as an instrument of power. The story of the girl and the cherry tree exposes a typical parent/child hierarchy and within the framework of this hierarchy the possibility of the child as knower or seer is eliminated altogether. There is no exchange, no meeting; only the parent who monopolizes the art of knowing and transforms it into mockery so as to maintain the superior role. The message to the girl is that she does not know anything and never will. The relationship between the Fool and King Lear, on the other hand, takes hierarchical traditions into its own hands. In normal circumstances the Fool, as court jester, would be one of the lowest of the King's subjects. In fact, at the beginning of the play, he has to show extreme caution so as not to offend his sovereign overmuch with his implications of the truth. However, as the situation worsens, an equality develops between them of a deeply emotional and intuitive nature. Both end up having to deal with the same physical extremes and in the process all sense of hierarchy is stripped away. As the Fool's teachings penetrate deeper, the King comes to realize how much true caring comes with them. He is then able to show caring in return and consider the welfare of a human being other than himself for the first time in his life. The Fool never came to the King professing to know. If he had, it is clear that no changes would have taken place. Instead he finds a way with seeming nonsense to move behind the protective masks and touch a softness of response that the King never knew he owned. He helps the gentle, giving part of the King to find life again, the part that nobody else can see, and stays with it through all extremes until the man is able to make contact with it himself. He remains committed to what his intuition tells him and takes whatever role is required for his knowledge to break through. He gives the King his true self back again without ever telling him directly what to do, or even giving him a sense of whether he knows himself, from moment to moment, how it will all turn out. He improvises as he goes along, letting each discovery lead to the next, joining him in every kind of emotional turbulence that is required for the masks to keep falling away. And once they are all down, the tenderness of the King's sensitivity can be revealed for both of them to see. Sensitivity can join with sensitivity and the real relationship between them can begin.

In the final sense, this is all that matters. Sensitive nature opening to sensitive nature to find out, in the fullness of meeting, what kind of exchange is really there. Over the rest there is no control; whether, in the process, we live or die, love or hate, make a deep connection or let each other go. But the differences and the range of potential within us all have to make themselves known; they have to announce themselves loud and clear in the face of all kinds of pressure to conform. Then the creator in us all can move in and merge with the sensitivity's recovered awareness, merge also with the vast array of emotions that are finally, along with that awareness, allowed to come flooding in.

XIV. FEAR, ANGER, HURT & PASSION

Emotions throw the being into disorder. They exist for that purpose and change cannot go very deep unless they gain free access to the body and recover their natural domain. If they gain access, they have the power to break down all structures that do not belong. They will take the design into their own hands and mould it according to their will with no regard for any other authority. Emotions are the sensitive nature's natural companions, and as the grounding in reality asserts itself, they will be sure to have their say. They are the unmistakable signs of a full life returning.

Most important is that they be given unlimited space to reenter the system. Sometimes emotions need to blast their way through with great force, particularly if they have been held under pressure inside for a long time. After years of discouragement they must be given a wholehearted welcome, received without judgment and, if possible, without fear. They have so much to tell that cannot be told in any other way. The mind can perhaps prepare for their entry, or even help in assimilation afterwards, but it has no capacity to embrace the full depth of experience in the moment nor can it articulate what it has been like for the body to have been deprived to such an extreme degree.

The new reality that the sensitivity joins with sends shock after shock wave through the system, and it is only the emotions that can loosen the physical body sufficiently in the face of so much change. Without the willingness of their support the body cannot open to receive what it has to receive. And if it does not open, everything freezes into resistance, refusing the information that wants to come through. Emotional release is a way of enlarging the arena of operations, and that enlarging process is taken seriously. The physical body may appear, at times, to be breaking apart under the force of the invasion, but this is only the body's way of demanding more room, demanding that it no longer exist as the small-scale vehicle for expression to which it has been reduced. It is a call to a fuller dimension, a challenge to step all the way forward into our largeness and take on the world from there. All in all, a finely-tuned sensitivity takes up a lot of space when the emotions are allowed to come along for the ride.

But to free them, to loosen them into the true form of their expression, is no easy matter. Often they have forgotten their original role as free-flowing agents. They have either retreated altogether from the scene, resigned to their own rejection, or they have become fixed lines of defense to ensure that the wounded core of sensitivity does not undergo any more pain. To deal with the stress, they have isolated themselves in the form of emergency weapons, firing in automatic repetitive patterns at the first sign of alarm; while their original intention was to act as feeling instruments with a continuous interchange and flow throughout all the centers of the body. Mostly they have been condemned as perpetrators of too much life and so do everything to disguise the degree of their aliveness and their potential impact on the outside world.

(II)

Emotions are particularly difficult to write about. Words are not their primary medium, and they resist attempts at being defined. Their natural form of expression is sound fully embodied, the kind of sound that takes one completely by surprise in the moment of expression, sound that takes over spontaneously with a range of volume, pitch and tone that the vocal chords have never imagined exploiting before. To talk about them can never do full justice to their power, yet located as they are at the heart of change, they have to be addressed somehow.

So consider, for a moment, the phenomenon of fear. The

earliest response to being alive is often fear. In fact, a baby in the process of taking on physical form is bound to be afraid because the world is a strange and sudden place to come into. It is not the existence of fear that is the problem, but people's responses to it: whether they respect its signals and offer comfort where comfort is due, or whether they override them and carry on as if they had never been. One thing is certain: by the time the baby is full grown there are clear signs as to how these first feelings have been received. The adult's behavior gives the information away.

For example, take a man who comes into a new situation and is completely at ease. He engages with other people immediately and talks with great confidence about any number of things. He is articulate; whatever comes up, there is a ready response at his command. The effect is smooth and certain in a way that resolves all doubts effortlessly. Now there are certain individuals who genuinely possess this kind of seamless confidence, but I believe that they are very rare. More often than not, this absence of fear is a mask to cover over what was not allowed to be felt as a child. It can be a somewhat disturbing phenomenon, this absence of fear, because it has such an attractive veneer. For some it may be inhibiting, but for others it can act as powerful inspiration because they are given the impression that life's problems are resolvable after all, particularly once a certain degree of knowledge is attained. There are seldom signs of physical stress in this kind of person, so thoroughly has the cover-up been accomplished; therefore it is hard to imagine that such knowing has been won at a price or that fear has at some early point been eradicated from this man's life. Its very absence betrays the possible extremes of childhood experience and how it has likely been forced underground to ensure a smooth passage through life. Furthermore, if his fear is missing, other extreme emotions are likely to be missing also, and unless the original experience of fear can be lured out of hiding, the expressive range of his life will never be complete. His fearlessness is locked in like a wide ring of protection around everything else he might feel, keeping him at a distance from close relationships with other people as well as from his own passion.

Very different from this is the fear which, despite all repressive efforts, has refused to go underground. This is a fear that takes over the body completely, screaming out in its desire for release, but kept rigidly under control at the same time. The result is a form of possession, leaving no space for any other feeling to come in. For a person entering a new situation in this state almost anything is acceptable, just so long as this internal panic does not erupt and risk some kind of public display. In this case the physical evidence is more telling, no matter how determined the control. The eyes, for example, are usually very wide open and the breathing shallow, giving the voice a resonance that is tightly strung. The movements are likely to be quick and angular, while any attitude of rest will be hard to find. It is as if the being has been struck in one single moment of terror, frozen in its initial response and unable to find release from it or move on. The fear, inexpressible at the time, has kept growing larger inside, clamoring for some kind of completion; for only a scream or a wail or even the possibility of retaliatory violence will release the system into the next feeling phase of its life. The possession will not end until the paralysis is broken and the original cause of such terror is made known.

Although these examples are very different, they are both evidence of early fear responses completely unreceived. Less common by far is the evidence of a child comforted; a child who has been encouraged to claim its fear and now, as a man, can be served by his emotions in a natural flow. The main difference is that alternatives of action are possible. If this man comes into a new situation for the first time, he can respond to it in a number of ways according to how safe he feels. If he feels immediately in danger, he can turn around and leave. If he feels uncertain, he can act warily, engaging to some degree and keeping in touch with the safety waves as they rise and fall. Or, if he feels completely at ease, he can let his wariness go altogether and engage openly. When each one of these options are open to him, his fear is serving him well. It can scan and shift by degrees, thereby providing essential information on an ongoing basis and letting him know accurately whether or not the environment is in his favor. Furthermore, his fear supports his sensitivity, opening it to potential nurturing or closing it off from potential harm. He might even have the choice of announcing his apprehensions out loud, provided this admission would be sympathetically entertained. In this way he shows that fear does not have to be masked as a thing of ignominy and shame, as it was in the first example. The emotion is available to himself, admissible to others, and above all things, flexible in its response to all interactions. It is in constant ebb and flow according to changing circumstances, able to give way to or join with other emotions if they should want to come in at any time and contribute their versions of the story.

The fear response of a small child is instinctive, a natural protection for a sensitivity that is delicate and unable to fend for itself. In order to foster this natural response, the child needs support from a sensitivity that matches its own, that becomes immediately aware of the smallest gestures or sounds of fear that the child shows towards a given situation. If these signs are respected and the expression of them allowed all the fullness they require, then the child learns to appreciate that the sensation of fear is a boon, a feeling to be depended on as reliable company on all new adventures. If, however, these signs are ignored, fear becomes trapped in the body, running in ever-increasing charges up and down the nervous system. Handling this fear becomes a full-time occupation, an all-consuming concern that severely limits the child's capacity to embrace life in an open way. Fear, from then on, will dominate, preceding all new situations like a portent of doom. This leaves the child with two alternatives: either to live with and attempt to control these physical extremes that keep taking the body over, or to numb them all out, cut off all feeling responses from the inside and find ways of engaging non-stop in the outside world. These last are the children who learn how to absorb themselves in all sorts of external accomplishments, becoming experts in anything so long as they are not reminded of the unacknowledged fears they once had to endure.

Both ventures involve skillful, long-practiced control. Through automatic reflexes they ward off the unpredictable in life, shunning extremes and all influences that disturb the **status quo**. As far as they are concerned, emotions only cause trouble and the result is a form of avoidance that can go on for years. Release or acknowledgement of this fear is like a watershed, a process of being plunged into the deep and subtle currents of the emotional world, a part of the self that is likely to run amuck for a while until the feelings are reinstated as the major catalyst of change.

(III)

If sufficient safety is built up over time for fear to take on its true function and if the body is allowed to throw itself around as it needs to do, then a whole network of emotional feeling is revealed. These feelings have been hiding behind the fear and are likely to take up defensive action where the fear has failed. When they assume that kind of emergency position, they take on a very fixed form. Anger, for example, in its fixed form is a particularly intransigent emotion. On first approach it behaves like a guard dog trained to attack at the slightest sign of danger. If fear lets go, it will be there instantly, ready to take on all comers, impeding any further advance. It forms the next layer of protection, making sure that the hurt is kept safe from harm, the hurt that was inflicted on the sensitivity many years ago, the wounds that have already gone deep into the heart. This hurt cannot yet take the risk of exposure, particularly now that fear's resistance has broken down, and so uses anger as a second line of defense, as insurance against complete disintegration.

Or, depending on the nature of the individual, it can be played out the other way around. It can happen that hurt, rather than anger, is the first to let itself be known, in an equally fixed and defensive form. It will cry out in pain and seem to find release, but soon a whining, repetitive tone will take over, circling round within itself and refusing to move on or give way to any other level of feeling. This is the form of hurt that insists it can do nothing about itself, insists that it is wounded beyond repair and no amount of attention will give it sufficient opportunity to heal. In this fixed state it serves the same purpose for the anger as the anger does for the hurt. It acts as a shield to prevent the rage from finding movement, making sure that it does not storm through in a ruthless and uncaring way.

Whichever way it happens, the most powerful emotional center will still remain hidden while the one acting in defense will show only a limited range. Besides, neither has the freedom of independent action. By mutual agreement, it would seem, they can only show themselves in the role of each other's protector and so their identity as single, moving agents remains in disguise.

When not in its attacking mode, anger, for example, can become a powerful source of energy and support. It is an expression of commitment that has no equal, proof of passionate concern. This is the aspect of anger that a child rarely has a chance to exercise; it is too direct and clear in its response, in the way it shows deep caring for some people and indignant outrage towards others. Anger, in this instinctive form, chooses without hesitation and is given to the child so that it will not be intruded upon by those people and circumstances that are not to its liking. Unfortunately the clarity of that anger, once it is expressed, is usually confronted by a different kind of anger in return, by an anger that wants to control and dominate as parent to child. This sets up a power struggle that the child, on the physical level alone, can only lose. The natural impulse towards anger is then replaced by fear, and as the anger disappears, so also disappears the child's innate capacity to look after its own interests, to speak of its commitment to the truth, to act freely and make choices in accordance with its highly developed perceptive powers. To find a way through life with a finely tuned sensitivity is hard enough, but to be deprived of anger in the process is to be stripped of substance, force and grounding all at the same time.

In the same way, if hurt can budge from its repetitive despair and learn that someone else exists in full understanding of its suffering, it begins to play to a very different tune. In its fixed form it complains unendingly about the heart's misery, whereas its true expression has to do with the infinite number of ways the heart can be affected and moved. When people have been battered, they cannot convey accurately what it means to be touched. They lose a sense of the subtler range of sensation, the difference, for example, between one person's form of contact and another's. Every move towards them risks the possibility of injury, and so there is no opportunity to consider what may exist besides. But when the extreme of pain is released, the possibility of intimate connection re-enters again, connection in which loving does not always have to be accompanied by pain. Ease in relationship is impossible when the hurt is that entrenched because the heart cannot expand, cannot open wide enough to let the pain pass through and out the other side. Once the loving and the pain are separated, however, the heart relieves itself of its burden and makes room for all the other sensations that have previously been turned aside.

The overall result is that these interdependent emotional layers become free-moving with expansive functions of their own. They get a chance to exercise themselves, flex their muscles and find their appropriate balance and flow. For example, anger as attack and anger as passionate commitment have very different styles. The first is a one-way street. It is a focused, single line of energy that moves out in a straight line towards an external target without any opportunity to change its shape or find out the deeper source of its identity. It fires out an automatic response before the individual has any idea of where the impulse is coming from. The second is a spiral that expands as it goes out and returns to the self in a continuous circulation of energy. At any point in its course it can change its nature, open as it is to draw from other emotional tones. It could transform into laughter, into tears, into the depths of despair. In fact, its main purpose in launching out is to find out the true nature of its expression, find out what it is connected to on a deeper level of the being. When it moves in this way, it throws everything up in the air, eager for some kind of change but never knowing, from one moment to the next, how all the pieces are going to fall. However they fall, as long as the anger is given full rein, the pattern will not be the same as before. It will have served its purpose by breaking through all the rigid, repetitive cycles of feeling; for its real strength comes from its ability to affect change to its own advantage, not from its capacity to defend and destroy.

This changing face of anger makes it possible for hurt to relax and find courage again. In anger's new identity it has support that it was always meant to have. If it knows that anger, rather than protecting the wounds of the past, can now move in before the wounding begins, it can open to new alternatives of action. It is not that anger, even in its fullness, can ever do away with pain. On the contrary, as the sensitivity continues to ground itself more firmly in reality, pain becomes an increasingly unavoidable element of life. The anger is not there to eliminate the pain, but to alleviate it, to make it finally bearable enough for the heart to receive its blows and not be overwhelmed, to let the pain pass through and respond from the greater depth that it has not been able to risk until now. The heart has a surprising resilience; and as soon as that resilience is given confidence again, it will find the capacity to connect with people on many different levels at the same time. But it cannot do this unless the anger is there to give it added strength and is ready to come to the rescue when trouble becomes too extreme. Love without anger is unlikely to move in very deep or survive very long. The territory of loving is uncertain at the best of times, and it is difficult to sustain the depth of exploration required without making use of anger's power to erupt and bring about sudden change.

When hurt and anger learn to cooperate in this way, a new

emotional flexibility comes into being. They can move in and out of each other in a constant fluid motion, opening or closing according to the situation and exchanging responses to what is going on around them. And when they find their right rhythms again, they are likely to move at great speed, a pace of operation very different from what the body has been used to: in one moment, out the next, a variety of moods chasing each other through, bringing together combinations of feelings that have not been put into operation before. For once the lines of resistance fall away, the moods multiply. These core emotions have not only given a false impression of themselves, but, in their wounded condition, they have hogged the scene so that neither the more delicate coloring of life nor the more positive extremes have had a chance to show. Without the release of anger there can be no ecstasy; without the release of pain, little capacity to take on the fullness of joy. Once fear has become unfrozen, it makes room for a long-starved curiosity that activates all the colors and details and makes out of them a veritable kaleidoscope of life.

(IV)

At the center of this complex emotional network is passion. The newly awakened curiosity in itself leads to passion. Anger, hurt, joy, ecstasy are all a part of it also. Passion is the force, the fluid energy, on which the natural rhythms of life ride. It is where all emotional streams merge, finding a central flow only when all repressive order lets go its hold. In its course it sweeps away the remnants of what does not belong and reaffirms a spontaneous flow of living and creating.

Passion in its rawest state is the most inarticulate emotion of all. It has no form, no deliberate intention, only a burning desire to engage fully in the experience of life. As soon as the emotions are dishonored, however, this desire begins to die. The mind takes over, insisting on answers, substituting the intellect for the feelings in its need to take over control. It is the insistence on mental control that has to be exposed before true integration with passion can begin. The mind has to let go sufficiently to allow passion to become its foundation, the true force behind whatever it needs to say.

Recovery of this passion is a process that runs parallel to the sensitivity's alignment with the truth. As the forgotten details of life's design make themselves known, the passion has to return to merge with them. It is the core strength that has been missing for so long, the absence that has made life so difficult to endure. To have this strength of passion come back is to know that ample energy is available after all, no matter how hard the challenge of the new reality may appear to be. Passion is, in fact, what energizes the relentless, undying search for the truth.

Passion is also of the moment and calls for immediate action. It does not know past or future. So when the mind lets go enough to move into the present, allowing the passion to carry its inspiration, the creative impulse is sprung. This impulse finds it movement and expression for however long, then dissolves back into the flood of passion again. Each creative act is temporary, rising and falling to its own rhythms, but the passion that gives birth to it is a constant flow, containing within it the raw energy for any number of inspirations.

Just as the rediscovered truth provides the details through which life's script can be played out according to its true design, so the reactivated passion provides the energy through which the player can engage in it most fully. But it is the passion that leads the way knowing what is true without need for argument or explanation, informing without words. It is an instant unmistakable communication between the gut and the heart, a signal that enters in advance of any articulation of the mind, inviting all relevant emotions to speak up clear. Only after that has happened will the mind settle back to its more appropriate task of assimilating and reordering the emotional information given, joining the emotions rather than fighting them off, acknowledging that the truth will not be found without their deep and thorough cooperation.

There are remarkably few people who express themselves with true passion on a daily basis; who, in all they say, communicate an aliveness without reservation; who are fully involved in what means most to them, whether it be some grand project or the smallest of details like the shape of a cloud passing across the sky. There is nothing ostentatious about this way of being, yet there is no mistaking the impression it leaves far beyond the moment of meeting. It is a quality that brings immediate life to people and situations, inspiration that moves in and changes things before there is even any awareness that life was lacking or that change was required. This transformation seems to come about without obvious effort or intent, but there is no doubting its reality after the event nor the difference in those who have been affected by the power of its influence.

XV. OVER AND OVER AGAIN

Despite the vision of the fool healed and the possibility of feelings recovering their natural flow, let there be no idealism or misunderstanding here. Large and fertile though this territory may be, there are no short cuts on the journey through. It can take a very long time to sort out the truth, to return to its accurate and subtle point of view. There are many layers, many details to be taken into consideration, and the knots and tangles that have developed over the years can seem endless. The complex weave of events that make up the march of personal history can, under nurturing circumstances, be integrated smoothly; but when the conditions are unsupportive, the threads separate from one another, making impossible any completion of the design. Every life, like every work of art, has its own special design which remains intact on a core level no matter how thoroughly it has been interfered with. The sensitive nature may arrange a hasty retreat into the depths of the being, but at the same time from its place of hiding it longs for the time when close and deserving attention can be given. Although, when this quality attention first arrives, there is little evidence of any conscious design. The weave is in disrepair, and it is hard to imagine that it was once whole.

But evidence of that wholeness, however slender, does remain and will respond to loving care. Each layer of truth discovered corresponds to a thread of the original design and leads towards its integration. A pattern then emerges that is like no other, and it is the feeling of that pattern recovering its strength and beauty that is the most healing factor of all. A new sense of order is restored, an order without fixed form, order that is released from the inside and so naturally takes on a flexible quality. The result is a movingly poetic version of reality that originally got lost in all the confusion. This poetic version is one that takes on perpetual motion, reaching out tentatively for each appropriate detail and adding little by little to the intricacy of the design. It represents life finally working in its own favor, a delicate criss-crossing of sensations, revealing more and more subtlety as the search for the truth goes on.

Through all the highs and lows of this search it is the poetic understanding of life that remains constant, insisting as it does on the range of experience that must be recorded. It acts as a touchstone for the truth through the uncertainty of the search process. The search is bound to be haphazard at first because the being has gotten so far removed from its original source. From a distance it peers back into the clouded past and catches at isolated fragments which have become disconnected from the rest of the design. It is from a state of conflict that the being first engages with the remembered scene, trying to distinguish between warring angles of interpretation and all the different versions that have been imposed over the years. It is as if ghost writers came in uninvited and conjured up the scene as they imagined it to have been, misinterpreting key relationships and giving a boost to any aspect that might deny the true feelings of the child.

For this reason, before all those ghost writers can be persuaded to leave, before the original script has a chance to regather its true detail and tone, it is necessary to return to certain incidents of childhood again and again. With each return more details emerge from obscurity as evidence, but it is only gradually that the overall pattern is revealed. It is a slow process and a dramatic one also: a secret life unfolding, full of its own peculiar highlights, its own surprising twists and turns.

(II)

To illustrate more clearly the slow unfolding of this drama, and also as a way of bringing together much of the material I have touched on here, I have chosen to explore an incident from my own childhood. The memory first came to me fifteen years ago during the first phase of my healing and has been giving me shock after shock of recognition ever since. I keep being surprised at the fertility of its resources and the degree to which my innocence continued to block me from the child's version of what really went on. Most of all, it is a prime example of how long it can take a child to return completely to his own side.

Scenario

I am about four years old, sitting at a large kitchen table at breakfast time. My mother is standing over me, repeating the same question over and over again: "You did do it, didn't you? You did do it, didn't you?" This is not a question so much as an accusation. She has already made up her mind on what she thinks I have done, so there is nothing I can do about it but sit there and endure. Occasionally I protest that I have no idea what she is talking about, but it is a routine that continues morning after morning regardless of what I say. Her large presence stands over me, and the voice grinds me down ruthlessly first thing every day. I do not know how long this goes on. I have little sense of time because the repetition surrounds the episode with a surreal quality that joins all these breakfasts into one endless interrogation. Perhaps most marked in the feeling memory is the dread of anticipation each morning as I gear myself up for the next round. At the beginning I am strong and able, more or less, to hold my ground. I am still a relatively feisty child at this stage and besides, I know I am in the right. Then bit by bit my strength begins to ebb away. The force of her interrogation becomes increasingly relentless and I begin to lose my initial confidence. I become bewildered, shaking inside, and even begin to doubt the truth of my own denial. I am not certain anymore. Perhaps, after all, I really did this terrible thing and should just admit to it and finish with the whole business. One morning it becomes too much. I cannot bear it any longer and I give in. I say, "Yes, I did do it." Afterwards all I remember is the relief pouring through. If there was punishment, I have no recollection of it; only release from a terrifying ordeal.

First Layer

When I first recovered this memory, I happened to be visiting family and mentioned it quite casually, almost jokingly, to my brother who is sixteen months older than I. To my surprise he remembered the incident also. It had stayed with him, he said, because of the guilt, because he had never confessed. He went on to inform me that he was the one who had done what my mother accused me of and had been afraid to own up to it in front of her. At the time I was not aware of the importance of this information, the fact that it deepened the effect of my memory and validated my innocence which, as far as I was concerned, was still very much in doubt. We laughed together about the absurdity of the situation and occasionally, during the following several years, I brought back the memory to ponder over it some more. Mostly I was puzzled. I could not understand how I had gained such a powerful reputation as a liar so early in my life. At four years old my mother had already identified me as the one who would be most likely to deceive her. What crimes, I thought to myself, must I have already perpetrated to gain such a terrible reputation, terrible enough for my mother to pounce on me immediately as the obvious culprit of any unadmitted wrongdoing. I wondered what had originally caused me to diverge so sharply from the truth, but came up with no satisfactory explanations. All I had was the mystery of myself as a prodigy liar, a strangely wayward and perverse child. My former behavior must have indeed been extreme for my mother to be so thoroughly wrong in her assessment of the situation. For the time being I left it at that.

Second Layer

When the memory returned some years later, it took on a very different guise. First of all, there was no room for reflection. It descended on me suddenly and emotionally, bringing along with it several other recently recovered scenes of my mother's behavior towards me. In fact, since the memory's first appearance, her identity had altered alarmingly, jolting me out of a long-time idealization. A disturbing sense of craziness hung in the air at that point in time, and I did not know whether the craziness was hers or mine. Certainly the foundations of our relationship were being severely undermined. As the scene played itself back again, it brought with it all sorts of disturbing sensations, a feeling of being caught up in some insane scheme of operation that was not, and never had been, of my own choosing. Rules, I was beginning to realize, were made up without my consent and were subject to change at a moment's notice; so my only recourse was to keep frantically adjusting to them to ensure a moment-to-moment survival. In all this emotional upheaval the visual details of the scene were much less clear. In fact, if I tried to focus on them for long, a feeling of nausea took over. However, one detail kept recurring: it was my mother's face as she interrogated me, bloated and grotesque as I had never seen it before. Until then whatever her mood, whatever the memory, I had always seen her as stunningly beautiful. It was difficult to accept that this leering face belonged to the same person.

Third Layer

Because this crazy, nightmarish version of my mother kept surfacing, I had to find the support of someone else to help me stay through it, to encourage me to confront the reality of her face in its new form. I had to find out what was behind it, and I could not do that alone. Even with this support I could not focus my attention for very long, but I gathered enough to get a first hit of the fanatical behavior I was being subjected to. To feel the extreme of it was to grasp that there were much larger issues involved than this crime that I had never even committed in the first place. The bottom line was a power play that was fierce indeed, a raw, head-on confrontation. For some reason my mother was out to get me. She was determined to impose her will on me, regardless of whether I had done wrong or not. Which meant that I was a threat to her, in some way that I did not yet understand. This new layer of emotional and physical response left no doubt about how large a threat I was and how much stake she had in putting me down. The certainty came from a powerful rushing in my body which, once contacted, radically changed the child's experience. It was literally turned upside down now that I was no longer assessing myself from my mother's point of view. Rather than identifying myself as a perverse child with a lying reputation, I felt her as a woman who would make anything up to suit her own fancy, anything so long as it would align with reality as she wanted it to be. The roles were reversed: now it was she who was the liar, not me. These harrowing confrontations at breakfast had been her chosen method of imposing her will on me, her way of breaking me early in life so that I would know, once and for all time, who was directing the show. It was at this point of discovery that my innocence began to loosen its hold. The moment I was able to accept that my mother was capable of behaving in this manner, I also accepted that this incident was, for all intents and purposes, the climax of a power game that had been going on ever since I was born.

Fourth Layer

Once the truth started to come through with this amount of force and conviction, it continued to gather more and more strength. Individual realizations joined together to form a larger whole. I had grown accustomed to a jumble of fragments around this issue and it was quite a revelation when the parts began to connect with each other to present a reality that was coherent and alive—alive from the child's point of view. The experience recovered its emotional identity from the inside and from then on each detail fell into place with surprising ease. For example, I understood why my brother, who had never acted before or since like a timid child, could not find the courage to tell my mother the truth. To present my mother with his knowledge of what actually happened would have meant setting himself up in direct opposition to the reality she was determined to impose. This information would not only expose her as being in the wrong, which would have caused enough trouble in itself, but it would have fouled up the larger scale of her operations, the role she had taken on so committedly as director of the family truth. He would have endangered his relationship with her on a very deep level and I am sure he was aware, however unconsciously, of the extreme of that risk. Also it became clear to me that he was not, and never had been, a threat to her in the same way I was, so there was no need for her to engage him in that form of confrontation. I speculate, given this more complete information, that it was not as a liar she had me branded, but as one who was likely to come out with uncomfortable truths at inappropriate times. And unless she broke me from that role, I would continue to challenge her edicts and sabotage the family control that was so important to her.

By the time I was unravelling this layer, I was in touch with a new feeling of expansion inside, very different from the self-degrading attitude that the memory had first invoked. I had shifted from allying myself with my mother's limited interpretation of my behavior to a penetration of the true dynamic between us. I struggled for a while with the question of whether she was conscious or unconscious in her actions, but eventually realized that it made no difference to my own experience either way. If she had done it consciously, I would only end up in a stuck place as victim, holding her to blame; while if she had done it unconsciously, I would slide back into the position of defending or excusing what could not be excused. Either way the attention would remain on her, and my own experience would be avoided again. It was the depth and complexity of my own experience that I needed to own, thereby finding out the true nature of the child I had been before I was waylaid into performing for someone else's script. To feel that this memory had strength to offer rather than weakness was to gather essential information about the original quality of my sensitivity, to catch glimpses of what it was like before such harsh limitations were imposed.

Fifth Layer

There is one more stage, one that continues in operation to this very day. It has to do with the way these realizations branch out and illuminate other episodes in my life. This is the stage where consciousness becomes constant movement, and the poetic impulse of life keeps furthering its own design. Through all the previous layers this memory, although increasingly suggestive and alive, still remained isolated within its own time frame. But in taking on its own life, it has reached out instinctively towards other experiences also, particularly those that shared the same emotional ground. The truth, once found in one area, will announce its return by encouraging other connected incidents to become clear also. In fact, it was only by re-examining other episodes with my mother that this particular incident opened so wide. The ricochet effect was already working in my favor as I moved further in, and I developed even more momentum as I moved out the other side. The connection was to several other childhood incidents, but one in particular is worth telling in some detail, if only because the link it offered finally put to rest one of the most humiliating and crazy-making experiences of my life.

In this scene I was ten years old at a boarding school for boys. It was part of the rigid routine at this school that everyone lined up at the beginning of recess for a daily bottle of milk. One particular morning I lined up as usual, but when I reached the head of the line I passed by without taking my milk. It was not that I had a strong distaste for the stuff; I just decided to change the routine on the spur of the moment, despite the fact that, from the moment of the decision, I knew I was getting myself into big trouble. After some time had passed, casual announcements were made through the halls that someone had not drunk his milk and would whoever it was go and claim his bottle immediately. These announcements increased in intensity and frequency, but despite my growing apprehension, I still made no move to improve my situation. A form of paralysis took me over, combined with an accelerating panic as I became aware of how the situation was careening out of control. The panic built as the commands became harsher, yet I was still unable to go to my own rescue. Eventually the whole school was denied recess and forced to sit at their desks in silence until the culprit confessed. I lasted an unbearably long time, long enough to extend my agony to the fullest possible extreme. Finally, in a breathless, terrified voice, I admitted my guilt and was hauled off to the Headmaster's office before the eyes of every boy in the school and thrashed.

The most striking aspect of this scene when I link it up with the earlier one is the pattern of repetition. I recreated on a public scale the ruthless assault of prolonged interrogation that my mother had inflicted on me six years previously. But there is one essential difference: the first time I was completely innocent, while the second time I fabricated my own guilt. I composed for myself the worst scenario imaginable, an accumulation of every agonizing detail as guarantee that my humiliation would be complete. The first incident was not of my creation at all; it was my mother's. I was dragged into her reality as an unwilling participant. The second, when it is linked to the first, appears to be an attempt to replay the situation so that the punishment is in alignment with the crime, so that the values inverted by my mother could find their rightful place again. Because of the earlier incident, I believe that truth and falsehood became impossibly confused inside of me. The distortion became so deeply embedded that I had to adopt drastic measures for the balance to be restored; or if not that, I had at least to enter blindly into the original confusion on my own terms and see if it would lead to a more appropriate resolution. At any rate, I am certain that the second incident would not have happened without the first. For all the humiliation of the school episode, what disturbed me most and continued to disturb me for a long time afterwards, was a belief that I was going insane. My terrified thoughts insisted that I must be totally crazy to bring down such untold horrors upon myself to no purpose. Because even though I predicted right away the impending disaster, I did not have control over my actions for one moment. The whole thing completely ran away with me, and there was no telling the insanity of what would follow.

When I made the connection between these two episodes, the relief was enormous. It constituted the final healing of my fear of insanity that had pursued me with varying intensity throughout my childhood. And that age-old fear was softened by a surprising compassion. The boy who had been harassed by his mother made himself known to the terrified boy at school and showed him the extent of his wounds, the extreme of what he had already endured, and therefore the reason why he had to engineer for himself such a grotesque scheme of suffering. In a case like that the understanding itself is a precious comfort indeed. It charts in feeling form compassionate explanations for otherwise bewildering and inexplicable events.

XVI. THE LARGER FRAME

All that I have dealt with here, this deep plunge inside to regather our individual resources, has only become possible in recent years. What is available now to me was not accessible to my parents and would have been quite incomprehensible to their parents before them. The challenge of being alive at this time is that we can know ourselves in a way that past generations could not. The language of the self is excitingly new; its power to bring about a large-scale change is newer still. Things are changing so fast internally that it is impossible for our present imaginations to take in the scope of who we are to become. We cannot even look to other people, whether older or younger, for any idea of what a fully realized identity can be. It is an intriguingly open-ended prospect, quite different from what my parents would have experienced as they looked towards the future from the midstream of their lives. Their imaginations were never able to embrace change with ease anyway, so certain structures were settled on immediately to ensure that radically new concepts would not be entertained. It is strange to look back on that time because they were revered as large and charismatic figures, which indeed they were. Yet they both died early giving up on life long before they became really large, that is, as large as it was possible for them to become. It appears in retrospect that they had nowhere to go to renew themselves, no more open roads to travel on; and so the vitality of their exploring energy died away. They also did not have enough of their inner beings to feed on, deriving strength instead from structures outside themselves, structures that had been handed down from generation to generation without discrimination and without thought for the vastly different individuals involved.

Despite recent changes, this need for outer form is still

surprisingly strong. The so-called New Age seems to be always on the brink of preaching yet another religion and when under stress the most common question people still ask is "so what should I do?" Radical changes are happening inside of them, and they still ask that question, which informs me that even those who are in touch with their inner process cannot keep pace with the power of its influence or understand how little it associates itself with "doing" anything. Because this course of discovery is so new, doubts are inevitable; and when they appear, it is the need for a set program that immediately reasserts itself, a desperate call for some infallible guarantee. In fact, there may be those who have read the book this far, have reached the final chapter, and are still looking for some well-ordered plan through which to apply these ideas systematically to everyday life. But the inner being does not work that way. It will give information, provided space is allowed for listening and entering into what the information provides. It will also help to reconnect the life-lines that have been broken and create its own order out of this new design. But those life-lines are completely individual and would justifiably resist whatever plan for their welfare I felt inclined to impose. Sooner or later they would resist because the levels of subtlety, which are in a constant process of recovery, would become too intricate to be held to any kind of set method or routine. In a sense it is the opposite that is involved here: the more the inner being is consulted, the more often fresh alternatives appear which, in a natural progression, move increasingly further away from the need for structured support. This finally marks the distinction between existence and survival; it is the art of existing, the invigorating fluidity of the dance, that we are being asked to engage in now, regardless of how few models there are from the previous generation.

However, there was one model I did have, an aunt who made all the difference. She was always the member of the family I was most attracted to as a child and that attraction made even more sense when she finally expressed to me in a long letter, only a few years ago, what she had experienced as a young woman growing up in her own generation. She described to me how she had slowly become aware of a "future generation" being born. As children she had been able to identify them by their unusual degree of sensitivity and by the fact that nobody knew what to do with them or how to come to terms with their unusual needs and desires. She identified them even then as new forms of energy and knew that none of the normal rules that were applied to children at that time would give them what they required. Even though she could see what was going on, she still had no idea as a parent or a woman what to do about it. She was herself a mother of five, yet she was as much at a loss as everyone else in regard to practical ideas of upbringing. My own sense is that she did much more than she knew. Her very awareness of the changes that were happening created a whole different tone within her own family, and I know that was why I loved to be with them. By creating this unusual, free-flowing atmosphere she was already preparing the way for this new kind of sensitivity and the influence it would have on the outside world. I got the impression from her letter that, as the future generation, we were born without a frame. The structures that had worked for previous generations had no function for us as a means of stability and learning. So, to all intents and purposes, we were left to our own devices, left to improvise and teach ourselves how we could best thrive. And in this hit-or-miss process there was little understanding and much pain.

The perspective my aunt gave me was both personal and far-reaching in its implications. It offered me the warm comfort of recognition as a child, but it also presented me with a sudden overview of this period of rapid change. The challenge, all at once, appeared very large: to give up thousands of years of reliance on the beliefs of others and trust that within the self there was enough information, and more, to go on; to accept that there could be no stable collective belief until its precepts were first connected to the inside and to all the eccentric characteristics that make us who we are. To understand that the differences came first, and only then would the unifying principles make themselves known. I also became more acutely aware of how much suffering the sensitivity had endured on this maiden voyage and what a long road of recovery lay ahead of it before it would be able to transmit, without interference, the new information necessary for the next aeon. It is about this suffering that I have primarily written because it feels so essential to come to terms with its extremes and be compassionate with the fears that still exist around exposing it to yet more pain. And it is in recognition of this long road of recovery that I have been devoted to finding for myself and for others the quality of support required so that the fears can be allayed and trust can return to its original foundations.

In addition to all this we have, stretching far behind us, a long heritage of brutal warfare during which the sensitivity of the individual nature has been completely overridden and denied. We are still staggering under the weight of that past and need as much time as possible to recover our balance, recover the subtle, creative strength that has been hidden, all this time, under the self-protective determination to destroy. There is an enormous difference between taking out our suffering on others and recognizing it within ourselves, and the difference will only make itself known if we immerse ourselves in the self's confusion and discover how much of our true strength we have been missing all this time. A transition period is, of necessity, a period of extremes, and the more that we take on the range of our identities as human beings, the more we can extend ourselves beyond imposed structures to meet those extremes. So life as passionless routine becomes a play of improvisation with the unknown.

To revel in the unknown is the foundation of our existence here, the adventure of breaking new ground. I described at the beginning how my sensitive nature, in its desperation to belong as a child, learned to adapt very soon, learned to be a chameleon to the outside world to cover up the strangeness of its ways. I end with that same sensitive nature founded on a different kind of adaptability altogether, an adaptability that connects to the inside and forms a stable base from which lightning changes can keep turning of their own accord. These changes have little to do with influences from the outside, little to do with fears of not being accepted by the mocking crowd. The impulse comes from the core and sets out at its own rhythm, in its own direction, with its own unique character and style.

A prison and a wild rose, side by side. A crying man curling into my arms. A girl, two years old, greeting rainbows with a peal of joy. A large man with cowboy boots watching an egret fishing from a stream. A cherry tree sprouting in the belly of a child. The Fool in the wilds of the storm. •

Stephen Francis Martineau has been teaching in various guises and many countries for over thirty years. He was raised in Scotland, went to New York for his doctoral degree, then to Canada to teach theatre at the University of Toronto. During this time he was drawn into an intense period of personal healing which became a more and more integral part of his work. Until eventually, in 1982, he moved to California where he established his own private practice. He works there with groups and individuals in his unique style, supporting people in the search for new aspects of themselves. He has travelled extensively and led groups in many different communities, including workshops in California, Hawaii, New York and Australia.

Mr. Martineau's next book, a fictionalized story of a woman's inner process through pregnancy and the birth of her child, is due to be published in the summer of 1993.